Qua Manifestation: Harnessing Physics for Self-Improvement

"Unlock the Secrets of the Quantum Realm to
Transform Your Life and Achieve Your Dreams."

Katherine Tope

Contents

Introduction

Chapter 1: The Quantum Mindset

Chapter 2: The Observer Effect

Chapter 3: Quantum Visualisation

Chapter 4: Quantum Action

Chapter 5: Quantum Resilience

Chapter 6: Quantum Connection

Conclusion

Before we start, let's grasp the fundamentals of quantum physics.

Step into the mind-bending world of quantum physics, where atoms dance and particles play by rules that defy our everyday intuition! Quantum physics is like a secret code that unlocks the mysteries of the universe at its tiniest, most intricate levels.

Imagine electrons and photons, those tiny building blocks of matter and light, behaving like both waves and particles at the same time! It's as if they're playing hide-and-seek with scientists, popping in and out of existence in the blink of an eye.

But that's just the beginning of the quantum fun! Ever heard of quantisation? It's like the universe's way of saying, "Hey, I only come in certain sizes!" Certain properties of particles, like their energy and momentum, can only have specific, fixed values, kind of like stepping stones in a game where you can only jump to certain spots.

And get this - in the quantum world, things can be in multiple places at once! It's called superposition, and it's like particles are doing a magical disappearing act, being here, there, and everywhere until someone decides to peek at them.

But wait, there's more! Picture this: particles becoming best buddies, no matter how far apart they are. It's called entanglement, and it's as wild as it sounds. What happens to one particle instantly affects its partner, even if they're light-years apart. Einstein called it "spooky action at a distance," and it's the stuff of quantum legends!

And just when you think you've got it all figured out, along comes the uncertainty principle. It's like the universe's way of saying, "Sorry, can't have it all!" Certain things, like knowing a particle's position and momentum at the same time, are a mystery, no matter how hard you try to measure them.

So buckle up and get ready to dive into the quantum rabbit hole, where reality is stranger than fiction, and every discovery is more mind-blowing than the last!

Introduction

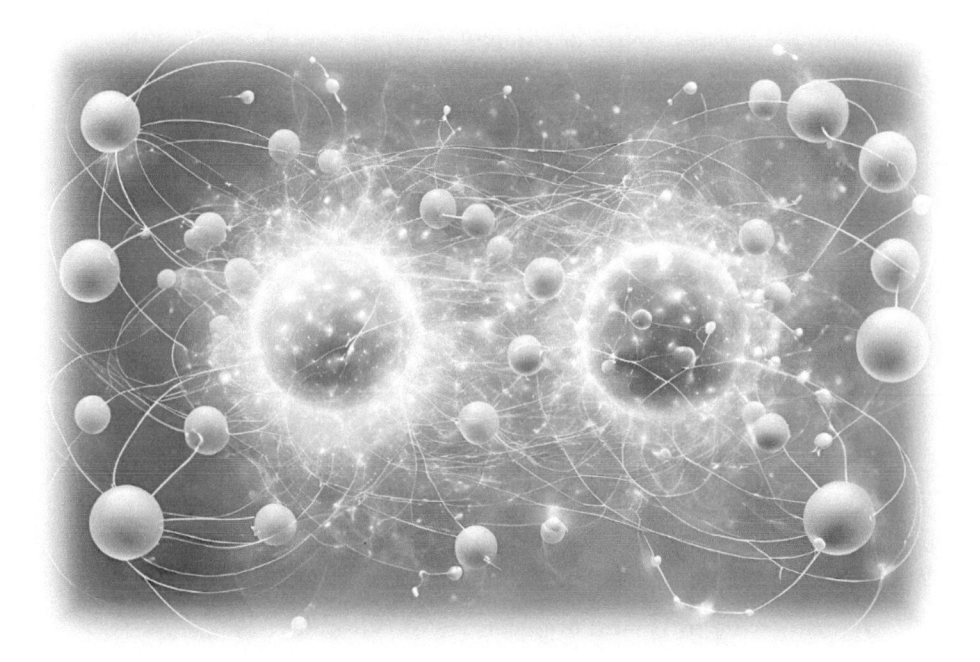

Welcome to the fascinating world of quantum manifestation, where the principles of physics converge with the art of personal transformation. In this introductory chapter, we embark on a journey through the realms of quantum physics, exploring how its foundational principles challenge our classical understanding of reality and illuminate new pathways for self-improvement.

At the heart of quantum physics lie three foundational principles: superposition, entanglement, and the uncertainty principle. These concepts, initially bewildering to those unfamiliar with quantum mechanics, hold the keys to unlocking a deeper understanding of the universe and our place within it.

Superposition, the first principle we encounter, defies the logic of classical physics by asserting that particles can exist in multiple states simultaneously. This concept challenges our conventional perception of reality, which is based on definite, observable states. Instead, it invites us to embrace a reality where possibilities are fluid and interconnected, where the potential for transformation is limitless.

Entanglement, the next principle we explore, introduces us to the notion of interconnectedness on a quantum scale. It suggests that particles can become correlated in such a way that the state of one particle instantaneously influences the state of another, regardless of the distance between them. This phenomenon challenges our classical

understanding of locality and separation, inviting us to consider the profound implications of our interconnectedness with the world around us.

The uncertainty principle, introduces an element of unpredictability into the fabric of reality. According to this principle, certain pairs of physical properties, such as position and momentum, cannot be precisely determined simultaneously. This principle introduces an inherent unpredictability into the fabric of reality, challenging the deterministic worldview of classical physics, suggesting that there are inherent limits to our ability to predict the behaviour of quantum systems.

As we delve deeper into the mysteries of quantum physics, we begin to see how these principles challenge our classical understanding of reality and open up new vistas for personal transformation. By embracing the fluidity of superposition, the interrelation of entanglement, and the potential of uncertainty, we can transcend the limitations of our classical conditioning and tap into a deeper reservoir of creativity, intuition, and resilience.

We will set off on a voyage into the depths of the quantum field, a realm where the potential for personal transformation knows no bounds. While, unravelling its mysteries and discovering the transformative power it holds for personal growth and manifestation.

The quantum field serves as the underlying fabric of reality, a vast and boundless sea of energy where all possibilities exist simultaneously. It is the fertile ground from which the universe emerges, a realm of infinite potentiality waiting to be shaped by the conscious observer. Within the quantum field, the past, present, and future are but different threads in the tapestry of existence, woven together in a dance of perpetual creation.

In this exploration, we look into the profound implications of the quantum field as the underlying fabric of reality. Here, all possibilities exist simultaneously, awaiting the guiding hand of consciousness to bring them into manifestation. This concept challenges our conventional understanding of reality as fixed and deterministic, inviting us to expand our perception and embrace a world of infinite potentiality.

Our thoughts and emotions play a pivotal role in shaping our experiences within the quantum field. Like ripples on the surface of a pond, they send out energetic vibrations that ripple through the fabric of reality, influencing the outcomes we attract into our lives. When we align our thoughts and emotions with our desires, we become conscious co-creators of our reality, harnessing the power of the quantum field to manifest our deepest aspirations.

However, this power comes with a caveat, our thoughts and emotions must be in alignment with our true desires. Just as a discordant note can disrupt the harmony of a symphony, negative thoughts and emotions can distort the energetic resonance within the quantum field, leading to outcomes that are out of alignment with our intentions.

As we journey deeper into the mysteries of the quantum field, we will learn how to harness its transformative power to cultivate a life of purpose, abundance, and fulfilment. We will explore practical techniques for aligning our thoughts and emotions with our deepest desires, empowering us to manifest our dreams with clarity and precision.

In the pages that follow, we will explore how these principles can inform and enrich our journey of self-improvement. We will learn how to harness the power of our thoughts, beliefs, and actions to manifest our desires and shape our reality in alignment with the principles of quantum physics. Together, we will embark on a transformative journey that promises to unlock new possibilities for personal growth and fulfilment.

I invite you to open your mind and heart to the wonders of quantum manifestation. Let us embark on this journey together, exploring the profound mysteries of the quantum realm and discovering the infinite potential that lies within each of us.

In the intricate dance of quantum manifestation, the role of consciousness emerges as a central protagonist. It is through the lens of consciousness that we navigate the quantum realm, shaping our reality with each observation and intention. In this book, we embark on a profound exploration of consciousness and its profound influence on the manifestation process.

At the heart of our inquiry lies the observer effect, a cornerstone of quantum mechanics that highlights the intimate relationship between consciousness and reality. According to this principle, the act of observation has the power to influence the behaviour of particles, collapsing their wave functions and determining their states. Through meticulous examination, we unravel the mysteries of the observer effect and uncover its implications for personal transformation.

Deeper still, we confront the profound question: How do our perceptions and intentions shape the fabric of reality? Drawing from both scientific research and spiritual philosophies, we embark on a multidimensional analysis of consciousness and its role in manifestation. From the pioneering experiments of quantum physics to the ancient wisdom of mystical traditions, we explore diverse perspectives on the nature of consciousness and its transformative potential.

We will encounter the remarkable parallels between the insights of modern science and the wisdom of spiritual teachings. Both converge on the profound truth that consciousness is not a passive observer but an active participant in the creation of reality. Through the power of our perceptions and intentions, we become co-creators of our experiences, sculpting our reality with each thought and emotion.

Yet, with great power comes great responsibility. We must tread the path of consciousness with mindfulness and discernment, for our perceptions and intentions shape not only our individual experiences but also the collective reality we share. Through conscious observation and intentional manifestation, we wield the power to co-create a world aligned with our highest aspirations, a world of abundance, harmony, and joy.

As we journey through the realms of consciousness and observation, let us cultivate a deeper awareness of the profound connection between mind and matter. Let us harness the transformative power of consciousness to manifest our dreams and aspirations, knowing that we are the architects of our reality, the weavers of our destiny.

Within the intricate tapestry of quantum manifestation, quantum entanglement emerges as an enchanting symphony of interconnectedness and synchronicity. As we unravel the mysteries of entanglement, we embark on a captivating exploration of the unseen threads that weave us into the very fabric of the cosmos.

At its core, quantum entanglement defies the conventional boundaries of space and time, linking particles in a state of profound correlation. Regardless of the distance separating them, entangled particles remain intimately connected, their states intertwined in a dance of exquisite harmony. Through meticulous examination, we look into the profound implications of entanglement for our understanding of the connections and synchronicity.

In our study, we encounter the remarkable parallels between the insights of quantum physics and the wisdom of ancient spiritual teachings. Both converge on the profound truth that we are interconnected beings, bound together by the invisible threads of entanglement. Through the lens of quantum entanglement, we begin to glimpse the underlying unity of all existence, a unity that transcends the boundaries of the individual self.

Venturing further into the realms of entanglement, we encounter the phenomenon of synchronicity – a phenomenon that defies rational explanation yet holds profound significance for our personal growth journey. Synchronicities are meaningful coincidences that seem to occur with uncanny frequency, guiding us along the path of our highest purpose. Through keen observation and interpretation, we learn to discern synchronicities as messages and symbols from the universe, offering guidance, insight, and affirmation on our voyage of self-discovery.

In our analysis of synchronicity, we encounter stories of serendipity. We discover the hidden patterns that weave through the tapestry of our lives, connecting us to a deeper, more meaningful reality. We learn to trust in the wisdom of synchronicity, knowing that every encounter, every coincidence, carries with it a message, a message that speaks to the inherent harmony and order of the universe.

As we embrace the profound interconnectedness of quantum entanglement and the transformative power of synchronicity, let us open our hearts and minds to the infinite possibilities that lie before us. Let us trust in the unseen forces that guide us, knowing that we are held in the loving embrace of the universe. And let us journey forward with courage and conviction, knowing that with each step we take, we are aligning ourselves more closely with our true purpose and highest potential.

In the labyrinthine corridors of quantum manifestation, the quest for healing and well-being takes on a extraordinary significance. As we navigate the intricate interplay between mind, body, and spirit, we unearth the transformative magic of quantum principles to rejuvenate and invigorate our existence.

At the forefront of this journey lies the burgeoning field of quantum biology, a realm where the boundaries between physics and biology blur, and the mysteries of life unfold. Through meticulous exploration of cutting-edge research, we unravel the hidden mechanisms that

orchestrate the intricate symphony of cellular processes and their profound impact on our health and vitality. From the quantum coherence of DNA to the ethereal vibrations of biomolecules, we uncover the profound entwining of the quantum realm with the realm of the living. Each discovery illuminates the intricate web of interconnectedness that binds us to the very essence of existence, inviting us to embrace the quantum mysteries that pulse within us all.

In our exhilarating exploration of quantum healing, we are enveloped in a vibrant tapestry woven from the threads of ancient wisdom and cutting-edge science, offering us profound revelations into the essence of healing itself. From the depths of energy medicine to the heights of vibrational therapy, we traverse a landscape brimming with transformative potential, learning to harness the dynamic power of quantum principles to nurture our physical, emotional, and spiritual well-being.

Through the kaleidoscopic lens of quantum healing, we behold the body not as a mere machine but as a dynamic masterpiece, endowed with the remarkable capacity to heal and rejuvenate itself. By attuning ourselves to the pulsating rhythms of the quantum field, we unlock the boundless reservoir of healing energy that courses through every fiber of our being. Through immersive practices like quantum visualisation, intention-setting, and energy healing, we awaken our body's innate healing intelligence, ushering in a symphony of harmony and equilibrium to every facet of our lives.

Yet, healing is not merely a physical process, it is a holistic journey that encompasses mind, body, and spirit. As we plunge deeper into the realms of quantum healing, we confront the emotional and spiritual dimensions of well-being, exploring practices such as mindfulness, meditation, and spiritual inquiry. Through these soul-stirring rituals, we cultivate inner peace, resilience, and self-awareness, laying the foundation for true and lasting healing to occur.

In our pursuit for quantum healing and well-being, let us embark on a riveting journey that intertwines the age-old wisdom of our ancestors with the groundbreaking insights of contemporary science. Weaving together the rich tapestry of ancient traditions and the cutting-edge discoveries of modern research, we forge a pathway towards a state of unparalleled wholeness and vitality.

As we stride boldly along this transformative path, let us reclaim the inherent power that resides within us, recognising the boundless potential nestled deep within the recesses of our being. With each step, profound metamorphosis and radiant health, traverses a luminous terrain with unwavering courage and steadfast conviction. As we press forward, let us remain fully focused that with every stride, we draw closer to embodying the vibrant, luminous beings we are destined to become.

Enter the captivating realm of Quantum Psychology and Mindset, where the intricate dance between consciousness and reality shapes the very fabric of our existence. Here, we embark on a journey into the depths of the mind, uncovering how quantum principles can illuminate the mind-body connection and empower us to cultivate a quantum mindset for boundless self-improvement.

At the core of Quantum Psychology lies a profound truth: the intricate interplay between mind and body, each influencing the other in a mesmerising dance of mutual influence and feedback. Drawing inspiration from the realms of quantum physics, we begin to grasp how our thoughts, beliefs, and perceptions sculpt the energetic landscape of our bodies, guiding the outcomes we attract into our lives.

Through meticulous examination, we unravel the enigmatic mysteries of the mind-body connection, looking into how quantum principles like superposition and entanglement shed light on the profound interdependence between mind and matter. Here, we uncover the transformative power of our thoughts—not mere fleeting mental constructs, but potent energetic vibrations resonating with the frequencies of our beliefs and perceptions, shaping our reality in alignment with their energetic signatures.

In our voyage through the realms of Quantum Psychology, we are introduced to the awe-inspiring potency of beliefs and perceptions—the very architects of our reality. Like master craftsmen crafting the blueprint of our experiences, our beliefs and perceptions construct the framework within which our existence unfolds. When we embrace empowering beliefs and nurture positive perceptions, we unlock the gates to a realm teeming with boundless opportunity and untapped potential. Conversely, when we cling to limiting beliefs and harbor negative perceptions, we unwittingly erect formidable barriers that obstruct the flow of abundance and joy into our lives.

Yet, the true essence of Quantum Psychology lies not merely in deciphering the inner workings of the mind, but in wielding practical tools and strategies to cultivate a quantum mindset for unparalleled self-improvement. Through the transformative alchemy of mindfulness practices, empowering affirmations, and cognitive reframing techniques, we can go on a profound journey of reprogramming our subconscious minds. In doing so, we align our thoughts and beliefs with the deepest desires and intentions of our hearts, propelling us towards the luminous horizon of our dreams.

Together, we shall embark on a riveting odyssey into the depths of the mind, where the enigmatic mysteries of Quantum Psychology intertwine with the sacred art of self-improvement. Here, amidst the fertile soil of boundless possibility and infinite potential, we shall unearth practical strategies for cultivating a quantum mindset. Let us journey forth, as we unravel the secrets of the universe and carve a path to create a world of boundless opportunity and infinite possibility.

Onto our journey into Quantum Manifestation Techniques, where the theoretical insights of quantum physics converge with practical strategies for transforming our desires into reality.

We will delve into a treasure trove of techniques for harnessing the power of quantum principles to manifest our deepest aspirations in every area of life.

At the heart of Quantum Manifestation lies the understanding that we are co-creators of our reality, actively shaping our experiences through the power of our thoughts, beliefs, and intentions. Drawing from the insights of quantum physics, we discover that the universe is a vast and responsive field of energy, eagerly awaiting our commands to bring our desires into fruition.

As we embark on an exploration of practical techniques for harnessing the power of quantum manifestation, we will begin with the transformative practice of visualisation. Visualisation is a powerful tool for aligning our thoughts and beliefs with our desired outcomes, allowing us to vividly imagine and emotionally embody the reality we wish to create. Through the practice of visualisation, we learn to immerse ourselves in the sensory experience of our goals, sending a clear signal to the universe and activating the law of attraction to bring our desires into manifestation.

Intention setting is another essential technique for quantum manifestation, empowering us to clarify our desires and focus our energy with precision and purpose. By setting clear and specific intentions, we create a roadmap for the universe to follow, guiding us toward our desired outcomes with effortless ease. Whether through written affirmations, spoken declarations, or silent intentions, the power of our intentions serves as a catalyst for transformation, aligning our thoughts, beliefs, and actions with the frequency of our desires.

But manifestation is not merely a mental exercise, it is a holistic process that encompasses mind, body, and spirit. Through the practice of energy alignment, we learn to attune ourselves to the vibrational frequency of our desires, harmonising our energetic field with the frequency of abundance and joy. Whether through practices such as meditation, breathwork, or energy healing, we cultivate a state of alignment and receptivity that allows our desires to effortlessly flow into our lives.

As we explore the intricate tapestry of practical techniques for quantum manifestation in depth, we will provide real-life examples and gripping case studies that vividly demonstrate their transformative prowess. Whether you seek to manifest abundance, love, health, or success, rest assured, these techniques offer a roadmap for unlocking the limitless potential that lies within you. So, brace yourself to unravel the mysteries that lie ahead and open your heart and mind to the endless possibilities that await. With every flicker of thought, every spark of belief, and every whisper of intention, you wield the power to sculpt the reality of your most cherished dreams.

Next, will be the exploration of Quantum Ethics and Responsibility, where the noble principles of integrity, authenticity, and ethical stewardship intersect with the profound art of manifestation. Here, we venture into the ethical underpinnings of quantum principles, uncovering how we can wield the power of manifestation in harmony with our deepest values and ideals for the greater good.

At the core of Quantum Ethics lies the recognition that with great power comes great responsibility. As co-creators of our reality, we wield the transformative power of quantum manifestation, shaping our experiences and outcomes with each thought, belief, and intention. Yet, amidst our pursuit of personal growth and success, it becomes imperative to pause and reflect on the ethical ramifications of our actions, recognising the ripple effects they create in the world around us.

We will begin by examining the importance of integrity and authenticity in the practice of manifestation. Integrity serves as the cornerstone of ethical behaviour, guiding us to align our thoughts, beliefs, and intentions with our highest values and principles. When we act with integrity, we honour the inherent dignity and worth of all beings, recognising that our actions have ripple effects that extend far beyond ourselves.

Authenticity, too, plays a crucial role in the practice of manifestation, inviting us to embody our true selves and express our deepest desires with honesty and sincerity. When we embrace authenticity, we tap into the power of our unique gifts and talents, allowing our true essence to shine forth and attract experiences that are in alignment with our highest purpose.

But ethical responsibility extends beyond our individual actions, it encompasses the collective impact of our thoughts, beliefs, and intentions on the world around us. As conscious co-creators of our reality, we bear a sacred duty to wield our power for the greater good, aligning our manifestation practices with values of compassion, empathy, and social justice.

Throughout our odyssey, we shall unveil practical strategies for nurturing ethical responsibility in the practice of manifestation. Whether through acts of kindness, service to others, or advocacy for social change, we have the power to make a positive impact on the world around us. By aligning our manifestation techniques with higher values and principles, we can harness the transformative power of quantum physics to create a world that reflects our deepest aspirations for peace, harmony, and justice.

Embrace the ethical imperative of quantum manifestation, knowing that with each thought, belief, and intention, you have the power to shape a reality that reflects the highest aspirations of humanity. Let us journey forward with integrity, authenticity, and ethical responsibility, knowing that by doing so, we are co-creating a world of beauty, abundance, and joy for all beings.

Step into the captivating realm of Quantum Evolution and Collective Consciousness, where the journey of self-improvement converges with the collective evolution of humanity and the planet. Here, we embark on a transformative journey into the interconnected realms of individual and collective consciousness, exploring how quantum principles can inform our understanding of social change, activism, and global transformation.

At the core of Quantum Evolution lies the recognition that we are not isolated beings but interconnected threads in the tapestry of existence, each contributing to the collective evolution of humanity and the planet. Drawing from the insights of quantum physics, we discover that the evolution of consciousness is an inherent aspect of the human experience, offering us boundless opportunities to expand our awareness and embody our fullest potential.

As we explore the role of individual and collective consciousness in shaping the evolution of humanity and the planet, we recognise that the choices we make as individuals ripple out into

the collective consciousness, influencing the trajectory of social change, activism, and global transformation. Through acts of compassion, kindness, and service to others, we contribute to the upliftment and evolution of humanity, creating a ripple effect of positive change that reverberates throughout the world.

But the odyssey of quantum evolution extends far beyond individual actions—it encompasses the collective awakening of humanity to its interconnectedness and inherent unity. As we recognise the profound interconnectedness of all beings and embrace the principles of unity and compassion, we begin to co-create a world that reflects the highest aspirations of the human spirit.

Prepare to explore practical strategies for catalysing collective evolution and social change. Whether through acts of kindness, advocacy for social justice, or participation in community-building initiatives, we have the power to make a positive impact on the world around us. By aligning our actions with higher values and principles, we can harness the transformative power of quantum physics to create a world that reflects the highest aspirations of humanity.

Let us embrace the journey of quantum evolution and collective consciousness, knowing that with each thought, belief, and action, you are contributing to the collective evolution of humanity and the planet. Let us journey forward with courage, compassion, and a commitment to social change, knowing that by doing so, we are co-creating a world of beauty, abundance, and joy for all beings.

As we welcome the final chapter of our Quantum Manifestation journey, we will reflect on the transformative potential of integrating quantum physics and personal development practices into our lives. In this chapter, we pause to contemplate the paths we've travelled, the lessons we've learned, and the infinite possibilities that lie ahead on our ongoing journey of exploration, growth, and self-discovery.

As we welcome the final chapter of our Quantum Manifestation journey, where we pause to marvel at the transformative fusion of quantum physics and personal development practices in our lives. In this chapter, we pause to contemplate the paths we've travelled, the lessons we've learned, and the infinite possibilities that lie ahead on our ongoing journey of exploration, growth, and self-discovery.

As we cast our gaze back upon the winding trails of our Quantum Manifestation expedition, we are awestruck by the profound metamorphosis brought about by intertwining quantum principles with personal development techniques. We've plunged into the enigmatic depths of quantum physics, peeling back the veils of mystery and unravelling its secrets, thus creating the life of our dreams. Through practical methodologies, we've harnessed the potent force of quantum manifestation, unlocking a kaleidoscope of possibilities for personal advancement and triumph.

But our journey doesn't end here, it is just the beginning of a lifelong exploration of the quantum realm and its transformative potential. Armed with optimism and curiosity, we embrace the perpetual quest for self-discovery and the infinite possibilities that lie ahead. We understand that the path of personal development is not always linear or predictable, but rather a dynamic and ever-evolving process of becoming.

We will continue to explore new horizons, deepen our understanding of quantum principles, and refine our manifestation practices. We will encounter challenges and obstacles along the way, but we will meet them with courage, resilience, and an unwavering commitment to our growth and evolution.

I encourage you to embrace the Quantum Journey Ahead with an open heart and a curious mind. Approach each day with optimism and enthusiasm, knowing that with each step you take, you are aligning yourself more closely with the radiant being you are meant to be. Embrace the challenges as opportunities for growth and celebrate the victories as milestones on your journey toward self-realisation.

As we embark on this Quantum Journey Ahead, let us do so with gratitude for the wisdom we have gained, the growth we have experienced, and the infinite possibilities that lie ahead. Together, let us continue to harness the power of quantum manifestation to create lives of joy, abundance, and fulfilment, knowing that the best is yet to come.

Chapter 1: The Quantum Mindset

Begin the transformative journey of The Quantum Mindset, where we explore the profound insights of quantum mechanics and their implications for personal growth and self-improvement. In this chapter, we embark on an exploration of the foundational principles of quantum mechanics, delving into how these principles challenge classical notions of reality and lay the groundwork for a new understanding of the universe and our place within it.

Introduction to Quantum Mechanics

In the vast and mysterious realm of quantum mechanics, the rules of classical physics give way to a strange and wondrous landscape governed by principles that defy our everyday intuitions. At the heart of quantum mechanics lie concepts such as superposition, wave-particle duality, and quantum entanglement, fundamental principles that revolutionise our understanding of the nature of reality.

Superposition, one of the cornerstone principles of quantum mechanics, challenges our classical notions of causality and determinism. According to this principle, particles can exist in multiple states simultaneously until they are observed or measured, blurring the lines between certainty and uncertainty, possibility, and actuality. This concept invites us to question the rigid boundaries of reality and consider the infinite potentiality that lies within each moment.

Wave-particle duality further expands our understanding of the quantum realm, revealing that particles can exhibit both wave-like and particle-like behaviour depending on the context of observation. This dual nature of matter challenges our classical distinctions between particles and waves, suggesting a deeper connectivity between all aspects of the universe.

Quantum entanglement, perhaps one of the most mysterious phenomena in quantum mechanics, describes how particles can become instantaneously connected, regardless of the distance separating them. This phenomenon suggests a profound interconnectedness between all particles in the universe, transcending the limitations of space and time.

As we journey deeper into the realm of quantum mechanics, we begin to glimpse a reality that is far more interconnected, dynamic, and participatory than we could have ever imagined. The principles of quantum mechanics challenge us to expand our minds and open ourselves to new possibilities for understanding the nature of reality and our place within it.

We will explore how these principles of quantum mechanics lay the groundwork for cultivating a Quantum Mindset, a mindset that embraces uncertainty, explores the realm of possibility, and harnesses the power of conscious intention to shape our experiences and outcomes. Together, let us begin on this transformative journey of exploration and discovery, knowing that with each step, we are aligning ourselves more closely with the radiant potential that lies within us.

Into the intriguing exploration of Quantum Reality and Consciousness, where we look into the profound relationship between our consciousness and the nature of reality. In this chapter, we look into what bridges the gap between science and spirituality, exploring how our perceptions, intentions, and consciousness interact with the quantum field to shape our experiences and outcomes.

Exploration of Consciousness and Reality

At the heart of the quantum realm lies the enigmatic relationship between consciousness and reality, a relationship that challenges our understanding of the world and invites us to reconsider the nature of existence itself. Drawing from both scientific research and spiritual philosophies, we begin to explore the role of consciousness in shaping our experience of reality.

Scientific research has increasingly recognised the fundamental role of consciousness in shaping our perception of the world. Studies in neuroscience and psychology reveal how our thoughts, beliefs, and emotions influence the way we perceive and interpret our surroundings, shaping our experiences and influencing our behaviour As we venture deeper into the mysteries of the brain-mind connection, we begin to unravel the intricate dance between consciousness and reality.

But the exploration of consciousness extends beyond the confines of scientific inquiry, it encompasses the realm of spirituality and metaphysics, where ancient wisdom traditions have long recognised the integration of all things. In spiritual philosophies from around the world, consciousness is viewed as the underlying fabric of existence, permeating every aspect of reality, and serving as the foundation upon which all experiences unfold.

The significance of consciousness in shaping our experience of reality becomes even more apparent when we consider the role of the observer effect in quantum mechanics. According to this principle, the act of observation has a profound influence on the behaviour of particles, suggesting that our consciousness plays a fundamental role in shaping the outcomes we observe. As we become aware of this interconnectedness between consciousness and reality, we begin to realise the immense power we hold to shape our experiences and outcomes.

The transformative exploration of the Quantum Mind-Body Connection, where we go into the intricate relationship between our thoughts, emotions, and physical well-being. As we embark on a journey of discovery, we explore the emerging research on the mind-body connection and uncovering how quantum principles can inform our understanding of holistic approaches to self-care and well-being.

Emerging Research on the Mind-Body Connection

In recent years, scientific research has increasingly recognised the profound influence that our thoughts, emotions, and beliefs have on our physical health and well-being. Studies in fields such as psychoneuroimmunology and epigenetics have shed light on the intricate interplay between mind and body, revealing how our mental and emotional states can influence the functioning of our immune system, gene expression, and overall health.

Through the practice of quantum manifestation, we begin to understand how our thoughts and emotions interact with the quantum field to shape our experiences and outcomes. Just as particles can exist in multiple states simultaneously, our thoughts have the potential to influence the energetic environment within our bodies, affecting everything from our cellular functioning to our overall health and vitality.

Holistic Approaches to Self-Care

But the mind-body connection extends beyond the physical realm, it encompasses the realm of spirit and consciousness, where the integration of mind, body, and spirit is essential for holistic well-being. Quantum principles can inform our understanding of holistic approaches to self-care, emphasising the importance of nurturing our mental, emotional, and spiritual health alongside our physical well-being. By adopting a holistic approach to wellness, individuals can achieve greater balance, harmony, and vitality in their lives.

Deepak Chopra: Integrating Mind, Body, and Spirit

Deepak Chopra, a renowned author and spiritual teacher, advocates for holistic approaches to self-care that encompass the integration of mind, body, and spirit. Through his books, lectures, and meditation programs, Chopra encourages individuals to nurture their mental, emotional, and spiritual health alongside their physical well-being. His holistic approach to wellness has inspired millions around the world to prioritise self-care and embrace a more balanced and harmonious way of living.

Yoga and Meditation Retreats: Inner Healing and Renewal

Yoga and meditation retreats offer participants a holistic approach to self-care, providing opportunities to nourish their mental, emotional, and spiritual well-being in addition to their physical health. Retreats often include practices such as yoga, meditation, mindfulness, and holistic healing modalities like Reiki or acupuncture. Participants emerge from these retreats feeling rejuvenated, refreshed, and more connected to themselves and their inner wisdom.

Holistic Health Centres: Integrative Healing

Holistic health centres offer comprehensive and integrative approaches to self-care that address the mind, body, and spirit. These centres often provide a range of services such as acupuncture, massage therapy, nutritional counselling, psychotherapy, and energy healing. By treating the whole person rather than just addressing symptoms, holistic health centres empower individuals to take an active role in their healing journey and achieve optimal well-being.

Nature Therapy and Ecotherapy: Healing in Nature

Nature therapy, also known as ecotherapy, emphasises the healing power of nature for holistic self-care. Success stories include individuals who have found solace, renewal, and healing by immersing themselves in natural environments such as forests, mountains, or bodies of water. Whether through hiking, gardening, or simply spending time outdoors, connecting with nature has been shown to reduce stress, improve mood, and enhance overall well-being.

Mindfulness-Based Stress Reduction (MBSR) Programs: Cultivating Awareness

Mindfulness-Based Stress Reduction (MBSR) programs offer evidence-based approaches to holistic self-care, focusing on cultivating present moment awareness and nonjudgmental acceptance of thoughts, emotions, and sensations. Stories include that the individuals who have participated in MBSR programs and experienced significant improvements in their mental, emotional, and physical health. By integrating mindfulness practices into their daily lives, participants learn to manage stress, reduce anxiety, and enhance overall quality of life.

Through practices such as meditation, mindfulness, and energy healing, we learn to cultivate a deeper awareness of the mind-body connection, allowing us to tap into the innate wisdom of our bodies and access our body's natural healing abilities. By aligning our thoughts, emotions, and beliefs with the frequency of health and vitality, we create an internal environment that supports our overall well-being and enhances our quality of life.

Discover the enlightening exploration of The Power of Thoughts and Beliefs, where we uncover the profound influence our thoughts and beliefs have on shaping our reality. We will investigate how the principles of quantum mechanics and the law of attraction converge to empower us to manifest our desires and unlock our true potential.

Understanding the Quantum Nature of Thoughts and Beliefs

In the quantum realm, thoughts and beliefs are not merely passive constructs of the mind, they are dynamic energies that shape the fabric of reality itself. Just as particles can exist in multiple states simultaneously, our thoughts and beliefs have the power to influence the outcomes we observe in our lives. Through the practice of quantum manifestation, we learn to harness the power of our thoughts and beliefs to create the reality of our dreams.

Drawing parallels between quantum mechanics and the law of attraction, we begin to understand how our thoughts and beliefs act as energetic frequencies that attract like-minded experiences into our lives. Like attracts like in the quantum realm, and by aligning our thoughts and beliefs with our desires, we can magnetise the experiences, opportunities, and resources needed to manifest our goals and aspirations.

Overcoming Subconscious Programming and Limiting Beliefs

But the path to manifestation is not always smooth, we are often hindered by subconscious programming and limiting beliefs that sabotage our efforts and hold us back from realising our full potential. We will explore how subconscious beliefs are formed and how they can act as barriers to personal growth and manifestation.

Through practical strategies such as mindfulness, visualisation, and cognitive reframing, we learn to reprogram the subconscious mind for success, replacing limiting beliefs with empowering beliefs that align with our goals and aspirations. By shining the light of awareness on our subconscious programming and actively engaging in the process of self-discovery and transformation, we can break free from the chains of the past and step into a future filled with possibility and abundance.

In this illuminating exploration of Quantum Intentionality, we dig deeply into the concept of intentionality in quantum physics and its significant role in manifestation and creative visualisation. A journey of discovery, exploring how to cultivate clear intentions and align them with the quantum field to attract desired outcomes and opportunities.

Understanding Quantum Intentionality

In the quantum realm, intentionality is not merely a passive desire or wish, it is a dynamic force that shapes the fabric of reality itself. Just as the act of observation influences the behaviour of particles in quantum mechanics, our intentions have the power to influence the outcomes we observe in our lives. Through the practice of quantum manifestation, we learn to harness the power of intentionality to manifest our deepest desires and create the reality of our dreams.

Examining the concept of intentionality in quantum physics, we begin to understand how our thoughts and intentions act as energetic frequencies that interact with the quantum field. Like

tuning into a radio station, our intentions broadcast a signal that resonates with similar frequencies in the quantum field, attracting like-minded experiences, opportunities, and resources into our lives.

Cultivating Clear Intentions

But the key to successful manifestation lies in cultivating clear intentions, intentions that are specific, focused, and aligned with our highest aspirations. We will explore practical strategies for clarifying our intentions and aligning them with the frequency of abundance and success.

Through practices such as journaling, visualisation, and affirmation, we learn to articulate our desires with clarity and precision, infusing them with emotion and passion to amplify their effectiveness. By bringing conscious awareness to our intentions and consistently aligning our thoughts, beliefs, and actions with our desired outcomes, we create a powerful vortex of manifestation that draws our goals and aspirations into our reality with effortless ease.

In this transformative examination of Quantum Resonance and Alignment, we investigate the profound notion of resonance and vibrational alignment within quantum physics and its implications for personal transformation. A journey of self-discovery, exploring how to raise our vibration and align with the frequencies of abundance, joy, and fulfilment through mindfulness practices, gratitude, and self-love.

Understanding Quantum Resonance

In the quantum realm, resonance is a powerful phenomenon that occurs when two or more frequencies synchronise and amplify each other's effects. Just as a tuning fork resonates with a specific frequency when struck, our thoughts, emotions, and beliefs emit energetic vibrations that interact with the quantum field. Through the practice of quantum manifestation, we learn to harness the power of resonance to amplify our intentions and attract like-minded experiences and opportunities into our lives.

Exploring the concept of resonance in quantum physics, we begin to understand how our vibrational frequency influences the reality we experience. When we are in vibrational alignment with our desires, when our thoughts, emotions, and beliefs are in harmony with the frequency of abundance and fulfilment, we create a resonance that magnetises our goals and aspirations to us with effortless ease.

Raising Your Vibration

But achieving vibrational alignment requires conscious effort and intention. We need to use practical strategies for raising our vibration and aligning with the frequencies of abundance, joy, and fulfilment.

Through mindfulness practices such as meditation, breathwork, and visualisation, we learn to cultivate a deeper sense of presence and awareness, allowing us to release resistance and align with the flow of life. By practicing gratitude and appreciation, we shift our focus from lack to abundance, inviting more blessings and opportunities into our lives. And by cultivating self-love and compassion, we elevate our vibrational frequency, aligning ourselves with the limitless potential that resides within us.

Enter the exploration of Quantum Interconnectedness, where we explore the deep comprehension of the interconnected nature of all things in the quantum realm and its significance for personal and collective consciousness. In this insightful journey of self-discovery and unity, we investigate how fostering a sense of interconnectedness and compassion can amplify our capacity to manifest our desires and contribute to the betterment of humanity and the world.

Understanding Quantum Interconnectedness

In the quantum realm, everything is interconnected at a fundamental level, a web of energy and information that connects all particles, objects, and beings in the universe. This interconnectedness extends beyond the physical realm, encompassing the realm of consciousness and spirit, where we are all part of the same cosmic tapestry.

Exploring the concept of quantum interconnectedness, we begin to understand how our thoughts, emotions, and actions ripple out into the world, influencing the collective consciousness and shaping the reality we collectively experience. Just as a drop of water creates ripples that spread across the surface of a pond, our individual contributions to the quantum field have far-reaching effects that extend beyond ourselves.

Cultivating Unity and Compassion

But the realisation of quantum interconnectedness invites us to transcend the limitations of the individual self and embrace a sense of unity and compassion for all beings. As we explore practical strategies for cultivating unity and compassion in our lives, knowing that by aligning ourselves with the greater good, we amplify our ability to manifest our desires and contribute to the well-being of humanity and the planet.

Through practices such as loving-kindness meditation, acts of kindness, and service to others, we learn to expand our awareness beyond the boundaries of the ego and connect with the inherent divinity within ourselves and all beings. By recognising the interconnectedness of all life and honouring the sacredness of each moment, we awaken to the infinite potential that resides within us and embrace our role as co-creators of reality.

Experience the Quantum Mindfulness and Presence, where we investigate the transformative power of mindfulness practices and their profound role in cultivating a quantum mindset. Through self-discovery and inner peace, we examine how mindfulness can help us observe our thoughts and emotions without judgment, enabling us to consciously choose our responses and create positive change in our lives.

Introduction to Mindfulness Practices

Mindfulness is the practice of bringing focused attention and awareness to the present moment, free from judgment or attachment to the past or future. Through practices such as meditation, breathwork, and present moment awareness, we learn to cultivate a state of inner peace and clarity that allows us to navigate life's challenges with grace and resilience.

We'll delve into the fundamental tenets of mindfulness and its significance in nurturing a quantum mindset. By grounding ourselves in the here and now, we establish a sanctuary of

inner calm and mindfulness that enables us to tap into the profound insights of our essence and harness our inherent wisdom and intuition.

Observing Thoughts and Emotions Without Judgment

One of the key benefits of mindfulness is its ability to help us observe our thoughts and emotions without judgment. In the quantum realm, observation plays a crucial role in shaping reality, and by cultivating a non-reactive awareness of our inner experience, we gain the power to consciously choose our responses and create positive change in our lives.

Through mindfulness practices such as meditation and present moment awareness, we learn to become the silent witness to our thoughts and emotions, observing them as they arise without getting caught up in their stories or dramas. In doing so, we create space for clarity and discernment, allowing us to respond to life's challenges with wisdom and compassion rather than react out of fear or unconscious habit.

Knowing that by anchoring ourselves in the present moment, we unlock the infinite potential that resides within us.

In the transformative journey of Overcoming Quantum Resistance, we probe into the typical hurdles and difficulties faced when embracing a quantum mindset. We will embark on a voyage of self-discovery and empowerment, examining tactics to conquer resistance and transition into a mindset characterised by openness, curiosity, and potential.

Exploration of Common Obstacles

As we journey toward embracing a quantum mindset, we inevitably encounter resistance, internal barriers that hinder our ability to embrace new perspectives and possibilities. Common obstacles such as scepticism, fear, and self-doubt can arise, casting doubt on our ability to manifest our desires and create positive change in our lives.

Throughout our voyage, we look into these obstacles with compassion and understanding, acknowledging their presence as natural facets of the human journey. By shedding light on our resistance with mindfulness, we carve out space for transformation and development, understanding that within every challenge lies an opportunity for enhanced self-awareness and empowerment.

Analysis of Strategies for Overcoming Resistance

But overcoming resistance requires conscious effort and intention. By implementing the following practical strategies, you can navigate the obstacles on the path to adopting a quantum mindset and cultivate a state of openness, curiosity, and possibility in your life.

Mindfulness Meditation: Engage in regular mindfulness meditation practice to cultivate present-moment awareness and develop a non-judgmental attitude towards thoughts and emotions. This can help you become more attuned to the present moment and open to new possibilities.

Positive Affirmations: Use positive affirmations to reframe limiting beliefs and cultivate a mindset of positivity and possibility. Repeat affirmations that align with your goals and aspirations to shift your mindset towards greater openness and curiosity.

Journaling: Keep a journal to explore your thoughts, feelings, and experiences, allowing you to gain insight into your beliefs and patterns of thinking. Journaling can help you identify and challenge limiting beliefs, fostering a more open and curious mindset.

Gratitude Practice: Cultivate a daily gratitude practice to focus on the positive aspects of your life and develop a mindset of abundance and appreciation. Recognising and expressing gratitude for the blessings in your life can shift your perspective towards greater openness and possibility.

Continuous Learning: Commit to lifelong learning and personal growth by seeking out opportunities to expand your knowledge and skills. Whether through reading, attending workshops, or taking courses, continuous learning can stimulate curiosity and open you up to new possibilities.

Embrace Failure as Learning: Shift your perspective on failure from a negative outcome to a valuable learning experience. Embrace failure as an opportunity for growth and self-discovery, allowing you to approach challenges with greater resilience and openness to possibility.

Visualisation: Practice visualisation techniques to envision your goals and desires as already accomplished. Visualising your desired outcomes in vivid detail can help you overcome obstacles and maintain a positive mindset, fostering a sense of openness and possibility.

Surround Yourself with Positivity: Surround yourself with supportive and positive influences, whether through relationships, communities, or media consumption. Surrounding yourself with positivity can help you maintain a mindset of openness, curiosity, and possibility.

Take Inspired Action: Take inspired action towards your goals and aspirations, trusting your intuition and inner guidance to lead you in the right direction. By taking proactive steps towards your dreams, you can overcome obstacles and manifest greater possibilities in your life.

Practice Self-Compassion: Be kind and compassionate towards yourself as you navigate challenges and setbacks on your journey. Practice self-compassion by treating yourself with

the same kindness and understanding that you would offer to a friend facing similar obstacles.

Through practices such as self-inquiry, reframing limiting beliefs, and cultivating a growth mindset, we learn to transcend the limitations of the ego and embrace the infinite potential that resides within us. By cultivating self-compassion and resilience, we create a foundation of inner strength and courage that allows us to face our fears and doubts with grace and confidence.

As we continue our journey of quantum manifestation and overcome resistance, we know that with each challenge we encounter, we are invited to deepen our understanding of ourselves and the world around us. The universe is conspiring to support us every step of the way.

In this insightful exploration of Embracing Quantum Evolution, we ponder the profound possibilities that come with adopting a quantum mindset and dedicating ourselves to personal evolution and growth. Throughout our journey of self-discovery and empowerment, we welcome uncertainty, change, and the innate wisdom of the quantum universe as guiding companions along our path forward.

Reflection on Transformative Potential

As we go through the realms of quantum manifestation, we are invited to recognise the infinite potential that resides within us, the power to shape our reality, transform our lives, and contribute to the evolution of consciousness. Embracing a quantum mindset is not merely a shift in perspective, it is a profound act of self-empowerment and liberation, freeing us from the constraints of limiting beliefs and inviting us to step into our highest potential.

Within these pages, we contemplate the transformative power held within adopting a quantum mindset. With each instance of presence, intention, and alignment, we actively participate in shaping the reality we desire. By embracing the concepts of uncertainty and change, we unlock boundless opportunities, where challenges serve as catalysts for growth and setbacks propel us closer to achievement.

Encouragement to Embrace Uncertainty and Change

But embracing quantum evolution requires courage and resilience. In a world that is constantly in flux, we are called to navigate the unknown with faith and trust in the inherent wisdom of the quantum universe. We will offer encouragement to embrace uncertainty and change, knowing that with each step we take, we are guided by the invisible hand of destiny.

Through practices such as surrender, letting go, and trusting in the process, we learn to release the need for control and surrender to the flow of life. By embracing change as a natural aspect of the evolutionary journey, we open ourselves to new possibilities and opportunities for growth, knowing that with each experience, we are evolving into the highest expression of ourselves.

As we continue our journey of quantum manifestation, let us use the transformative power of quantum evolution, knowing that with each moment of presence and intention, we are aligning ourselves with the radiant potential that lies within us. Together, let us trust in the inherent wisdom of the quantum universe and navigate the journey ahead with courage, grace, and an open heart, knowing that the best is yet to come.

Chapter 2: The Observer Effect

Welcome to the enlightening exploration of The Observer Effect, where we uncover the fascinating phenomenon that lies at the heart of quantum physics. Here, we will embark on a journey to understand the profound implications of the observer effect for our understanding of reality and consciousness.

Introduction to the Observer Effect

The observer effect is a fundamental concept in quantum physics that reveals the intricate relationship between the observer and the observed. At its core, the observer effect suggests that the act of observation can influence the behaviour of particles and systems, fundamentally altering the outcome of experiments and challenging our traditional notions of causality and determinism.

We will define and explain the observer effect, highlighting its significance in shaping our understanding of the nature of reality. By observing the behaviour of particles at the quantum level, scientists have discovered that the mere act of measurement can cause particles to behave differently than they would in the absence of observation, an astonishing revelation that defies our classical intuitions about the predictability of the physical world.

Exploration of Observational Influence

But what does this mean for our understanding of reality and consciousness? In this chapter, we explore how the observer effect extends beyond the realm of quantum mechanics, influencing our everyday experiences and perceptions of the world around us. Just as particles can exist in multiple states simultaneously until observed, so too can our reality be shaped by the focus of our attention and the intentions behind our observations.

By becoming conscious observers of our own lives, we gain the power to influence the outcomes we observe, shifting our reality in alignment with our thoughts, beliefs, and intentions. In this way, the observer effect invites us to recognise the profound role that consciousness plays in shaping our lived experience, empowering us to become active participants in the co-creation of our reality.

As we continue our exploration of the observer effect, let us embrace the transformative power of conscious observation, knowing that with each moment of awareness, we are shaping the fabric of reality itself.

In the enlightening exploration of Conscious Awareness and Intention, we look into the profound relationship between conscious awareness, intentionality, and the observer effect in personal development. In this exploration, we journey into self-discovery and empowerment, examining how our attention and intention can shape our reality, drawing from both scientific research and spiritual teachings.

Understanding the Relationship

Central to personal development lies the interplay between conscious awareness and intentionality, the conscious choice to direct our attention and focus on specific outcomes. Just as the observer effect in quantum physics suggests that the act of observation can influence the behaviour of particles, so too can our conscious awareness and intentionality shape the reality we experience.

Discussing the profound relationship between conscious awareness, intention, and the observer effect, recognising that our thoughts, beliefs, and intentions have the power to shape our lived experience. By becoming conscious observers of our own lives, we gain the ability to influence the outcomes we observe, aligning ourselves with the reality we desire to create.

Examination of Attention and Intention

But how do our attention and intention shape our reality? In this section, we investigate the mechanisms through which our thoughts and beliefs influence our lived experience, drawing from both scientific research and spiritual teachings. Through practices such as mindfulness, visualisation, and intention setting, we learn to harness the power of our attention and intention to manifest our desires and create positive change in our lives.

Scientific research has shown that the brain responds to our thoughts and intentions, rewiring itself in response to our conscious focus. Similarly, spiritual teachings emphasise the importance of aligning our intentions with our highest values and aspirations, recognising that our thoughts have the power to shape the reality we experience.

The illuminating exploration of The Power of Focus and Attention, where we look into the crucial role that focus and attention play in manifesting our desires and achieving our goals. Let's explore how directing our attention toward what we want to create, can amplify our manifestation efforts, and attract aligned opportunities and resources.

Understanding the Importance of Focus

At the heart of quantum manifestation lies the power of focus and attention, the conscious choice to direct our mental and emotional energy toward specific outcomes. Just as a magnifying glass focuses sunlight to create a beam of intense heat, so too can our focused attention magnify the manifestation of our desires, bringing them into sharper focus in our reality.

The importance of focus and attention in manifesting our desires, recognising that where our attention goes, energy flows. By directing our focus toward what we want to create, we align ourselves with the vibrational frequency of our desires, drawing them closer to us and activating the process of manifestation.

Discussion of Amplifying Manifestation Efforts

But how does focusing our attention amplify our manifestation efforts? Scientifically, the brain operates on a principle known as the Reticular Activating System (RAS), which filters information based on our beliefs and priorities, bringing relevant information to our conscious awareness. By directing our attention toward our goals and desires, we prime the RAS to filter for opportunities and resources that are aligned with our intentions, making it more likely for us to notice and seize them.

Spiritually, focused attention acts as a form of energetic alignment, signalling to the universe our commitment to our desires and activating the Law of Attraction, the principle that like attracts like. By consistently focusing our attention on what we want to create, we send a clear signal to the universe and begin to attract experiences, people, and resources that support the realisation of our desires.

The enlightening exploration of Mindfulness Practices for Observation, where we will go into the transformative power of mindfulness techniques for becoming conscious observers of our own lives. Over the next few pages, we will embark on a journey of self-discovery and empowerment, exploring how mindfulness can help us cultivate present-moment awareness, observe our thoughts and emotions without attachment, and consciously choose our responses.

Introduction to Mindfulness Techniques

Mindfulness is the practice of bringing our attention to the present moment with openness, curiosity, and non-judgment. It offers us the opportunity to become fully present in our experience, cultivating a deep sense of awareness and connection to the present moment.

As we acquaint ourselves with mindfulness techniques and methods to become conscious observers of our own lives, we can use practices like meditation, breathwork, and body scanning. These techniques enable us to ground our awareness in the present moment, facilitating clear and balanced observation of our thoughts, emotions, and sensations.

Explanation of Mindfulness Benefits

But why is mindfulness such a powerful tool for observation? By training our attention through mindfulness practices, we develop the capacity to observe our thoughts and emotions without attachment, allowing us to see them for what they are, transient phenomena arising and passing away in the field of consciousness. This perspective enables us to break free from habitual patterns of reactivity and unconscious behaviour, empowering us to consciously choose our responses and create positive change in our lives.

In the insightful exploration of Quantum Self-Reflection, we uncover the transformative practice of self-reflection as a means of observing our thoughts, beliefs, and behaviours. Here, we venture into a journey of self-discovery and empowerment, discovering how self-reflection can assist in identifying patterns, limiting beliefs, and areas for growth, empowering us to make conscious choices and initiate positive change.

Exploration of Self-Reflection

Self-reflection is the practice of introspection, a deep dive into the depths of our inner world to gain insight and understanding into ourselves. It is a sacred journey of self-discovery, inviting us to observe our thoughts, beliefs, and behaviours with curiosity, compassion, and non-judgment.

Through practices such as journaling, meditation, and introspective questioning, we learn to shine the light of awareness on our innermost thoughts and feelings, gaining clarity and insight into our true nature.

Analysis of Self-Reflection Benefits

But why is self-reflection such a powerful tool for personal growth and transformation? By engaging in regular self-reflection, we develop the capacity to observe our thoughts, beliefs, and behaviours with objectivity and detachment, enabling us to identify patterns that may be holding us back from realising our full potential. Through this process, we gain insight into the underlying causes of our challenges and struggles, empowering us to make conscious choices and create positive change in our lives.

Empowering exploration of Aligning Thoughts and Actions with Goals, where we look into the transformative practice of aligning our thoughts, beliefs, and actions with our goals and intentions to harness the power of the observer effect. Here, we engage in a journey of empowerment and manifestation, delving into practical strategies for setting clear intentions, visualising success, and taking inspired action toward our desired outcomes.

Discussion of Alignment

At the heart of quantum manifestation lies the power of alignment, the conscious choice to align our thoughts, beliefs, and actions with our goals and intentions. Just as aligning a telescope allows us to focus our vision on distant stars, so does aligning our thoughts and actions with our goals, so they can allow us to bring our desires into clearer focus in our reality.

Our focus here is on the significance of alignment in manifesting our desires. It's crucial to acknowledge that when our thoughts, beliefs, and actions are in sync with our goals, we trigger the observer effect, thereby influencing the outcome of our experiences.

Exploration of Practical Strategies

But how do we align our thoughts and actions with our goals? Setting clear intentions involves identifying what we truly desire and stating our intentions with clarity and conviction. Through practices such as journaling, visualisation, and affirmations, we clarify our goals and imbue them with positive energy and intention.

Visualising success involves vividly imagining ourselves achieving our goals and engaging all our senses to create a rich and immersive experience. By visualising success regularly, we prime our subconscious mind to recognise opportunities and resources that support the realisation of our desires.

Taking inspired action involves moving toward our goals with purpose and intention, trusting our intuition and inner guidance to lead us toward our desired outcomes. By taking consistent and aligned action, we demonstrate our commitment to our goals and open ourselves to receive the support of the universe.

In this insightful exploration of Overcoming Resistance to Observation, we study common obstacles and challenges that may arise when practicing observation and intentionality. Throughout this journey of self-awareness and empowerment, we examine strategies for overcoming resistance and staying aligned with our goals, even in the face of distractions, self-doubt, and resistance.

Examination of Common Obstacles

As we progress along the path of self-improvement and manifestation, we may encounter various hurdles that impede our ability to observe our thoughts and intentions with clarity and focus. These obstacles, spanning from distractions and self-doubt to resistance and fear, have the potential to obstruct our advancement and hinder our alignment with our goals.

In this section, we scrutinise the common obstacles and challenges that may arise when practicing observation and intentionality. By shedding light on these barriers, we gain insight into their nature and their impact on our ability to manifest our desires.

Analysis of Strategies for Overcoming Resistance

But how do we overcome resistance and stay aligned with our goals? Mindset shifts play a crucial role in overcoming resistance, as they enable us to reframe challenges as opportunities for growth and learning. By adopting a growth mindset and cultivating resilience, we build the inner strength and determination needed to overcome obstacles and stay aligned with our goals.

Accountability structures provide external support and encouragement, helping us stay committed to our goals and accountable for our actions. By enlisting the support of mentors, coaches, or accountability partners, we create a supportive environment that empowers us to overcome resistance and stay on track.

Self-care practices nurture our physical, mental, and emotional well-being, replenishing our energy and resilience in the face of challenges. By prioritising self-care activities such as meditation, exercise, and creative expression, we cultivate the inner resources needed to overcome resistance and stay aligned with our goals.

As we continue our journey of self-awareness and empowerment let's know that with each obstacle we overcome, we grow stronger and more resilient. Let us cultivate a mindset of possibility and perseverance, knowing that the path to our goals is paved with challenges that we are fully capable of overcoming.

The enlightening exploration of Cultivating a Daily Observation Practice, where we put into action the transformative power of incorporating observation and intentionality into our daily routines for personal development and manifestation. We will look into various techniques and exercises for cultivating a daily observation practice that aligns with our goals and aspirations.

Introduction to Daily Observation Practice

At the heart of quantum manifestation lies the practice of observation, the conscious choice to observe our thoughts, beliefs, and intentions with clarity and focus. By incorporating observation into our daily routines, we create opportunities for self-awareness, growth, and alignment with our goals.

Here, we introduce the concept of a daily observation practice for personal development and manifestation. We will show you how dedicating time each day to observe our thoughts, beliefs, and intentions can provide us with insight into our inner world and empower us to make conscious choices that align with our goals and aspirations.

Exploration of Techniques and Exercises

But how do we cultivate a daily observation practice? Journaling provides a powerful outlet for self-expression and reflection, allowing us to capture our thoughts, feelings, and insights in writing. By journaling regularly, we create a space for self-discovery and exploration, gaining clarity and perspective on our goals and aspirations.

Visualisation involves vividly imagining ourselves achieving our goals and desires, engaging all our senses to create a rich and immersive experience. By visualising our desired outcomes with clarity and emotion, we activate the creative power of our subconscious mind, paving the way for manifestation.

Meditation offers a sacred space for quiet reflection and introspection, allowing us to observe our thoughts and emotions with mindfulness and presence. By cultivating a regular meditation practice, we develop the capacity to quiet the mind, access our inner wisdom, and align with our highest intentions.

In this exploration, we uncover the transformative potential of our observations and intentions to contribute to the collective consciousness and influence larger-scale changes. Throughout this journey of collective empowerment and social transformation, we investigate the potential for collective manifestation through shared intentions, group meditation, and conscious activism.

Discussion of Collective Influence

As we journey along the path of personal development and manifestation, it's essential to recognise the interconnectedness of all beings and the collective influence we have on each other and the world around us. Our observations and intentions ripple out into the collective consciousness, shaping the reality we collectively experience.

We will engage in a thoughtful discussion of how our observations and intentions contribute to the collective observer effect. By recognising the power we hold as co-creators of our reality, we can harness the collective consciousness to manifest positive change on a larger scale.

Exploration of Collective Manifestation

But how do we harness the collective observer effect for manifestation and social transformation? Shared intentions are a potent catalyst for collective manifestation, as they align the energy and focus of individuals toward a common goal or vision. Through practices such as group intention-setting and collective visualisation, we amplify the power of our intentions and accelerate the manifestation process.

Group meditation offers a sacred space for collective healing and transformation, allowing individuals to come together in shared mindfulness and intentionality. By synchronising our breath and consciousness, we create a unified field of energy that radiates out into the world, bringing about positive change and harmony.

Conscious activism involves taking intentional action toward social and environmental justice, guided by values of compassion, equality, and sustainability. By mobilising collective efforts toward positive change, we can address systemic issues and create a more just and equitable world for all beings.

In our insightful exploration of Embracing the Power of Observation, we jump into the transformative potential of incorporating the observer effect into our lives, committing to a path of conscious awareness and intentionality. Throughout this journey of self-discovery and empowerment, we reflect on the inherent power of our attention to shape our reality.

Reflection on Transformative Potential

At the core of quantum manifestation lies the power of observation, the conscious choice to observe our thoughts, beliefs, and intentions with clarity and focus. By embracing the observer effect, we open ourselves to a world of infinite possibilities and potential for growth and transformation.

We can reflect on the transformative potential of embracing the power of observation in our lives. We recognise that by observing our thoughts and intentions with curiosity, openness, and compassion, we can gain insight into our inner world and make conscious choices that align with our highest aspirations.

Encouragement to Practice Observation

But how do we embrace the power of observation in our daily lives? We can offer encouragement and guidance for cultivating a practice of conscious awareness and intentionality.

We encourage you to practice observation with curiosity, approaching each moment with a sense of wonder and fascination. By observing your thoughts, beliefs, and intentions without judgment or attachment, you create space for self-discovery and growth.

We invite you to practice observation with openness, embracing the present moment with acceptance and receptivity. By being fully present and engaged in the here and now, you can cultivate a deeper sense of connection with yourself and the world around you.

We urge you to practice observation with compassion, extending kindness and understanding to yourself and others. By approaching each observation with empathy and compassion, you create a nurturing environment for personal growth and transformation.

As you embark on your journey of embracing the power of observation, remember that every moment is an opportunity for growth and expansion. Trust in the inherent power of your attention to shape your reality, and embrace the journey with courage, curiosity, and an open heart. Harness the transformative potential of observation and create lives of joy, fulfilment, and abundance.

Chapter 3: Quantum Visualisation

The enlightening exploration of Introduction to Quantum Visualisation, where we look into the transformative practice of harnessing the power of visualisation to manifest our desires. In this chapter, we embark on a journey of creative visualisation infused with quantum principles, discovering how the observer effect and the interconnectedness of all things can enhance our manifestation efforts.

Definition and Explanation

At the heart of quantum manifestation lies the practice of visualisation, the art of vividly imagining our desired outcomes with clarity and emotion. By engaging our senses and emotions in the process of visualisation, we activate the creative power of our subconscious mind, paving the way for manifestation.

Here, we define and explain quantum visualisation as a powerful technique for manifesting desires. We explore how visualisation goes beyond mere imagination, serving as a catalyst for transformation and manifestation in our lives.

Overview of Quantum Enhancement

But what sets quantum visualisation apart from traditional visualisation techniques? In this section, we provide an overview of how visualisation can be enhanced by incorporating quantum principles.

The observer effect teaches us that the act of observation can influence the behaviour of particles and systems. In the realm of visualisation, this means that our focused attention and intention have the power to shape our reality. By consciously observing and visualising our desired outcomes, we align ourselves with the infinite possibilities of the quantum field.

The interconnectedness of all things reminds us that we are not separate from the world around us, but rather intimately connected to it at a fundamental level. In the practice of quantum visualisation, this means that our intentions and desires are woven into the fabric of the universe, affecting not only ourselves but also the collective consciousness. By visualising our desires with a sense of interconnectedness and unity, we tap into a vast reservoir of creative energy and support.

In this insightful examination of Understanding the Creative Power of Imagination, we explore the profound role of imagination in the manifestation process and its capacity to bridge the gap between thought and reality. Here, we unravel the mysteries of quantum physics and how they propose that the mind has the power to shape and influence the material world through visualisation.

Exploration of Imagination's Role

Imagination is an extraordinary aspect of the human mind, enabling us to conceive of possibilities beyond our current reality. It functions as the conduit between our thoughts and the realisation of our desires, serving as the canvas upon which we depict our dreams.

Moving on, let's study an investigation of the role of imagination in the manifestation process. Imagine you're a sculptor standing before a block of marble. With each strike of your chisel, you chip away at the stone, revealing the form that exists within your mind's eye. Similarly, imagination acts as the creative force that materialises our desires, enabling us to envision and embody the lives we aspire to lead.

Consider the story of Sarah, a young woman with a passion for photography but trapped in a mundane office job. Each day, Sarah would close her eyes during her lunch break and visualise herself capturing breathtaking landscapes and captivating portraits. Through the power of her imagination, Sarah began to see opportunities where she once saw obstacles. She started taking evening photography classes, saving up for a professional camera, and networking with other photographers. Slowly but surely, Sarah's vision began to materialise. She landed her first paid gig, then another, until eventually, she was able to quit her office job and pursue photography full-time.

In Sarah's journey, imagination served as the spark that ignited her passion and fuelled her determination. By envisioning herself living the life she desired, Sarah was able to take inspired action towards her goals, overcoming challenges and manifesting her dreams into reality. Just like the sculptor who carves away at the marble to reveal the masterpiece within, Sarah used her imagination to sculpt the life she wanted to lead.

As we delve deeper into the role of imagination in the manifestation process, let Sarah's story inspire us to harness the power of our own imagination to envision and create the lives we aspire to lead.

Discussion of Quantum Influence

But how does quantum physics shed light on the creative power of imagination? Quantum physics teaches us that the observer effect, the act of observation influencing the behaviour of particles, extends beyond the realm of the quantum world and into our everyday experiences. This suggests that our thoughts and intentions have the power to shape and mould the world around us.

Visualisation, as a form of focused imagination, taps into this quantum influence by aligning our thoughts and emotions with our desired outcomes. By vividly imagining ourselves experiencing our goals and desires, we send a powerful signal to the universe, signalling our intentions and attracting corresponding experiences.

In this enlightening exploration of The Science of Visualisation, we uncover the empirical research and neurological mechanisms behind the efficacy of visualisation techniques for achieving goals and enhancing performance.

Here, we unravel the science behind visualisation, shedding light on how it activates neural pathways, primes the subconscious mind, and influences physiological responses.

Examination of Scientific Research

Scientific research has increasingly recognised the power of visualisation as a potent tool for achieving goals and improving performance across various domains of life. Here is where we conduct an examination of the existing body of research on visualisation techniques.

Studies have shown that athletes who engage in mental imagery, visualising themselves successfully executing their skills, often demonstrate improved performance compared to those who do not. Similarly, individuals who visualise themselves achieving their goals report greater motivation, confidence, and persistence in pursuing their aspirations.

Analysis of Neurological Mechanisms

But what are the underlying neurological mechanisms that make visualisation so effective? When we engage in visualisation, whether imagining ourselves acing a job interview or completing a marathon, our brain activates the same neural networks involved in actual performance. This primes our nervous system and muscles for action, enhancing our readiness to execute the desired behaviours when the opportunity arises.

Furthermore, visualisation stimulates the reticular activating system (RAS), a network of neurons in the brainstem responsible for filtering sensory information and directing attention. By repeatedly visualising our goals with clarity and emotion, we signal to the RAS that these outcomes are important, increasing our focus and awareness of relevant opportunities in our environment.

As we deepen our understanding of the science behind visualisation, we gain insight into its profound impact on our mental, emotional, and physiological well-being. By harnessing the

power of visualisation and aligning it with the principles of quantum manifestation, we unlock the limitless potential to create the lives we desire. Let us embark on the transformative journey of visualisation and quantum manifestation, knowing that with each visualisation, we are sculpting our reality and shaping our destiny.

Into the transformative exploration of Quantum Visualisation Techniques section, where we uncover practical methods for harnessing the creative power of visualisation to manifest our deepest desires. In this area, we initiate a journey of discovery, introducing guided visualisation exercises, mental rehearsal, vision boards, and creative visualisation scripts as powerful tools for quantum manifestation.

Overview of Techniques

Visualisation is a potent practice that allows us to vividly imagine our desired outcomes, activating the creative power of our subconscious mind and aligning ourselves with the quantum field. This is where we provide an overview of various visualisation techniques that can supercharge our manifestation efforts.

Guided Visualisation Exercises: Guided visualisation exercises involve following a recorded script or narration that leads us through a journey of vivid imagery and sensory experiences. These exercises help us to relax deeply, tap into our inner wisdom, and visualise our desired outcomes with clarity and emotion.

Mental Rehearsal: Mental rehearsal involves mentally practicing and rehearsing desired behaviours, actions, or outcomes in our mind's eye. By repeatedly visualising ourselves successfully achieving our goals, we prime our subconscious mind and enhance our readiness to take action when the opportunity arises.

Vision Boards: Vision boards are visual representations of our goals, dreams, and aspirations created through collages of images, words, and affirmations. By compiling images and words that evoke the feelings and experiences we wish to manifest, vision boards serve as powerful visual reminders of our intentions and goals.

Creative Visualisation Scripts: Creative visualisation scripts are written narratives or scripts that guide us through visualisation exercises, providing detailed descriptions of desired outcomes and experiences. These scripts help us to engage our imagination, evoke positive emotions, and align our thoughts and beliefs with our desired reality.

As we explore these quantum visualisation techniques, let us remember that the key lies in consistency, clarity, and emotional resonance. By incorporating these techniques into our daily practice, we amplify our manifestation efforts and bring our dreams to life with greater ease and grace.

In this illuminating exploration of Setting Clear Intentions for Visualisation, we discuss the pivotal role of intentionality in harnessing the transformative power of visualisation. Here, we examine the importance of setting clear intentions before engaging in visualisation practices and explore practical strategies for defining specific goals, clarifying desired outcomes, and creating a detailed mental image of success.

The Importance of Setting Clear Intentions

Setting clear intentions is fundamental to the success of any manifestation practice, including visualisation. Our intentions act as the guiding force that directs the focus of our thoughts, emotions, and actions toward our desired outcomes. Without clear intentions, our visualisation efforts may lack direction and efficacy, limiting their potential to manifest tangible results.

We emphasise the importance of setting clear intentions as the first step in the visualisation process. By clearly defining what we wish to manifest and articulating our goals with precision and clarity, we provide the subconscious mind with a specific target to aim for, increasing the likelihood of success.

Exploration of Goal Definition and Outcome Clarification

But how do we set clear intentions for visualisation?

1. Define Specific Goals: Begin by identifying the specific goals or desires you wish to manifest through visualisation. Whether it's achieving career success, improving relationships, or enhancing health and well-being, clarity is key. Clearly articulate what you want to manifest in your life, ensuring that your goals are specific, measurable, achievable, relevant, and time-bound (SMART).

2. Clarify Desired Outcomes: Once you've identified your goals, take the time to clarify the desired outcomes associated with each goal. Visualise in detail what success looks and feels like for each goal, engaging all your senses to create a rich mental image of the desired outcome. Imagine yourself experiencing the fulfilment of your goals with clarity, vividness, and emotion.

By setting clear intentions and clarifying desired outcomes before engaging in visualisation practices, we empower ourselves to focus our energy and attention on what truly matters to us. With each visualisation session, let us reaffirm our intentions, aligning our thoughts and beliefs with the reality we wish to create. Let's set forth on the journey of quantum manifestation with clarity, purpose, and unwavering determination.

Enter the captivating realm of Engaging the Senses in Visualisation, where we unveil the transformative power of integrating sensory experiences into our visualisation practices. In this segment, we explore how engaging the senses can amplify the effectiveness of visualisation and share practical strategies for infusing sensory details, emotions, and physical sensations into our visualisations to craft a more immersive and impactful experience.

The Power of Sensory Engagement

Our senses are powerful gateways to the subconscious mind, allowing us to access deeper levels of awareness and creativity. When we engage the senses in visualisation, we activate multiple neural pathways and amplify the emotional resonance of our experiences, making our visualisations more vivid, compelling, and effective.

Here we explore how engaging the senses in visualisation can enhance the effectiveness of the practice, allowing us to create a more immersive and impactful experience.

Incorporating Sensory Details

One of the keys to effective visualisation is the incorporation of sensory details into our mental imagery. By engaging all five senses, sight, hearing, touch, smell, and taste, we create a multi-dimensional experience that stimulates the subconscious mind and enhances the realism of our visualisations.

For example, when visualising a desired outcome, imagine the sights, sounds, and textures associated with that experience. Visualise the vibrant colours, intricate details, and panoramic vistas. Hear the sounds of success, the applause, the laughter, the words of encouragement. Feel the sensations, the warmth of the sun on your skin, the texture of the ground beneath your feet, the embrace of a loved one.

Incorporating Emotions and Physical Sensations

In addition to engaging the external senses, it's equally important to engage our internal senses, our emotions and physical sensations. Emotions are powerful energy currents that influence our thoughts and beliefs, shaping our reality in profound ways. By infusing our visualisations with positive emotions, such as joy, gratitude, and excitement, we amplify the vibrational frequency of our intentions and attract aligned experiences into our lives.

Similarly, pay attention to the physical sensations that accompany your visualisations. Notice the feelings of expansion, lightness, and vitality that arise within you as you visualise your desired outcomes. By tuning into these sensations, you strengthen the mind-body connection and anchor your visualisations in the present moment.

As we explore further into the practice of engaging the senses in visualisation, let us remember that the key lies in immersion, intention, and emotional resonance. By infusing our visualisations with sensory richness and emotional depth, we tap into the full potential of our subconscious mind and unleash the creative power of the quantum universe. Let us embark on a sensory journey of quantum manifestation, where every visualisation is a step closer to realising our dreams.

Onto the enlightening exploration of Overcoming Limiting Beliefs and Blocks, where we confront the common obstacles and challenges that may arise during visualisation and discover effective strategies for transcending them. In this fragment, we dive into the depths of our subconscious minds to unearth limiting beliefs and self-doubt, and we empower ourselves with transformative techniques to release resistance and clear the path to manifestation success.

Confronting Limiting Beliefs and Self-Doubt

Limiting beliefs and self-doubt can act as formidable barriers on the journey of manifestation, obscuring our vision and dampening our manifestation efforts. These beliefs, often ingrained in our subconscious minds through past experiences and conditioning, can manifest as thoughts such as "I'm not good enough," "I don't deserve success," or "I'll never achieve my goals."

We will confront these beliefs head-on, acknowledging their presence and understanding their origins. By shining the light of awareness on our limiting beliefs and self-doubt, we begin the process of unravelling their grip on our psyche and reclaiming our power to manifest our deepest desires.

Strategies for Overcoming Resistance and Releasing Blocks

But how do we overcome these barriers and clear the path to manifestation success? This is where we explore a variety of transformative strategies for overcoming resistance and releasing blocks, including:

1. Affirmations: Affirmations are powerful tools for reprogramming the subconscious mind and replacing limiting beliefs with empowering thoughts and beliefs. Create affirmations that counteract your specific limiting beliefs and repeat them daily with conviction and belief.

2. Reprogramming Techniques: Explore techniques such as Neuro-Linguistic Programming (NLP), Emotional Freedom Techniques (EFT), and hypnotherapy to reprogram your subconscious mind at a deeper level. These techniques can help you identify and release subconscious blocks and rewire your neural pathways for success.

3. Mindset Shifts: Cultivate a growth mindset by reframing challenges as opportunities for growth and learning. Practice self-compassion and self-love, recognising that setbacks and failures are natural parts of the manifestation journey. Adopt an attitude of resilience, perseverance, and optimism in the face of adversity.

By implementing these strategies with consistency and dedication, we can gradually dissolve the barriers of limiting beliefs and self-doubt that stand in the way of our manifestation success. With each affirmation, each reprogramming session, and each shift in mindset, we reclaim our inherent power as creators of our reality and pave the way for the manifestation of our deepest desires.

Enter an insightful passage of Integrating Quantum Visualisation into Daily Practice, where we uncover the transformative potential of incorporating visualisation into our daily routines to reinforce intentions and maintain focus. In this area, we explore the practical strategies and rituals that can help us infuse our daily lives with the power of quantum visualisation, guiding us towards greater alignment with our desires and intentions.

Harnessing the Power of Routine

Routine is the backbone of consistency and discipline, providing structure and stability to our daily lives. By integrating quantum visualisation into our daily routines, we create dedicated time and space for nurturing our intentions and aligning our thoughts with our desired outcomes. Whether it's through morning rituals, visualisation breaks throughout the day, or evening reflections, routine acts as a catalyst for transformation, amplifying the effectiveness of our visualisation practice.

Morning Rituals: Start Your Day with Intention

Begin each day with a powerful morning ritual that sets the tone for manifestation success. Dedicate a few moments upon waking to engage in visualisation exercises that align with your goals and intentions for the day ahead. Visualise yourself embodying the qualities of success, abundance, and fulfilment, and feel the emotions associated with achieving your desires. By starting your day with intention and clarity, you prime your mind and spirit for manifestation success.

Visualisation Breaks: Infuse Your Day with Intention

Throughout the day, take short breaks to engage in quick visualisation exercises that reinforce your intentions and maintain focus. Whether it's during your lunch break, a moment of downtime, or before important meetings or tasks, steal a few moments to close your eyes and visualise your desired outcomes with clarity and conviction. By infusing your day with intentional visualisation breaks, you keep your goals at the forefront of your mind and stay aligned with the quantum field of potentiality.

Evening Reflections: Review and Reinforce

As the day draws to a close, take time to reflect on your experiences and accomplishments. Review the progress you've made towards your goals and acknowledge any insights or revelations that have emerged throughout the day. Engage in a final visualisation exercise before bed, visualising yourself drifting off to sleep in a state of deep relaxation and alignment with your desires. By ending your day with reflection and visualisation, you reinforce your intentions and invite the universe to work its magic while you sleep.

Incorporating quantum visualisation into your daily practice is a powerful way to maintain focus, reinforce intentions, and cultivate alignment with your desires. By infusing your routines with the transformative power of visualisation, you create a harmonious synergy between your inner world and outer reality, paving the way for manifestation success. Embrace the daily practice of quantum visualisation as a catalyst for personal growth, empowerment, and manifestation mastery.

Enter the illuminating adventure of Quantum Visualisation for Manifestation, where we uncover the profound impact of visualisation on manifesting our desires. Here, we reveal real-life examples and success stories that illustrate the transformative power of quantum visualisation, demonstrating how this practice can attract aligned opportunities, resources, and synchronicities to bring our goals to fruition.

The Power of Visualisation in Action

Visualisation is more than just a mental exercise, it is a dynamic tool for harnessing the creative power of the mind to shape our reality. Throughout history, countless individuals have used visualisation techniques to manifest their dreams and achieve extraordinary success in various fields, from sports and business to personal development and spirituality.

Real-Life Examples of Visualisation Success

Explore inspiring real-life examples of individuals who have used visualisation to manifest their desires and overcome seemingly insurmountable obstacles. From athletes visualising victory on the field to entrepreneurs envisioning the success of their businesses, these stories demonstrate the remarkable impact of visualisation on performance, confidence, and goal achievement.

Athletic Achievement: Olympic athletes often use visualisation techniques to enhance their performance. For instance, Michael Phelps, the most decorated Olympian of all time, famously visualised his races in detail before competing. By mentally rehearsing every stroke and turn, he primed his body and mind for success, leading to his remarkable achievements in swimming.

Career Success: Many successful professionals credit visualisation for helping them achieve their career goals. Oprah Winfrey, for example, visualised her success as a talk show host and media mogul long before it became a reality. By envisioning herself thriving in the entertainment industry, she attracted opportunities that eventually led to the creation of her own television network and immense influence in the media world.

Health and Healing: Numerous individuals have used visualisation to aid in their healing journeys. One notable example is Anita Moorjani, author of "Dying to Be Me." Anita experienced a miraculous recovery from end-stage cancer after a near-death experience. During her illness, she practiced visualisation techniques that focused on her body's innate ability to heal itself. This shift in mindset and visualisation of health contributed to her remarkable turnaround.

Entrepreneurial Success: Entrepreneurs often use visualisation to manifest their business goals. Steve Jobs, co-founder of Apple Inc., famously visualised the company's success and innovation long before it materialised. He envisioned Apple products transforming the way people interacted with technology, and his unwavering belief in this vision propelled the company to become one of the most influential in the world.

Personal Growth and Happiness: Many individuals use visualisation to manifest personal growth and happiness. Author and speaker Tony Robbins advocates for the power of visualisation in his seminars and books. He encourages people to vividly imagine their desired outcomes and to embody the emotions associated with achieving those goals. Through consistent visualisation and action, individuals can attract aligned opportunities and experiences that contribute to their overall fulfilment and well-being.

Analysis of Visualisation Mechanics

How does the mechanics of visualisation work to manifest our desires? By vividly imagining our desired outcomes with all our senses, we send a clear signal to the universe and activate the law of attraction, drawing aligned opportunities, resources, and synchronicities into our lives. Visualisation acts as a powerful magnet, aligning our thoughts, emotions, and actions with our intentions and paving the way for manifestation success.

Attracting Aligned Opportunities and Synchronicities

As we consistently engage in visualisation practices, we begin to notice a subtle shift in our reality as aligned opportunities, resources, and synchronicities effortlessly present themselves. These serendipitous occurrences are not mere coincidences but rather manifestations of our focused intention and alignment with the quantum field of potentiality. By staying open and receptive to these signs and guidance, we further accelerate the manifestation process and bring our goals to fruition with ease and grace.

Incorporating Visualisation into Your Manifestation Journey

Armed with the knowledge and inspiration from these real-life examples and insights, you are now equipped to harness the power of visualisation for your own manifestation journey. Whether you're seeking to improve your health, advance your career, or deepen your relationships, visualisation can serve as a potent catalyst for transformation and manifestation. Embrace this practice with enthusiasm and dedication and watch as the universe conspires to support you every step of the way.

Embracing the Creative Power of Visualisation, where we immerse ourselves in the profound impact of quantum visualisation on personal growth and manifestation. Here, we reflect on the transformative potential of this practice and offer encouragement to cultivate a daily visualisation practice with consistency, patience, and faith in the creative power of the mind.

Unlocking the Potential Within

Visualisation is a gateway to unlocking the limitless potential that resides within each of us. By harnessing the creative power of the mind, we can transcend perceived limitations, overcome obstacles, and manifest our deepest desires. Through visualisation, we access the quantum field of infinite possibilities and align our thoughts, emotions, and actions with our intentions, paving the way for profound transformation and manifestation success.

A Daily Practice of Empowerment

Cultivating a daily practice of visualisation is an act of empowerment, a commitment to consciously co-create our reality and manifest our dreams. By dedicating time each day to visualise our desired outcomes with clarity, intention, and emotion, we strengthen our connection to the quantum field and amplify our manifestation efforts. With consistency, patience, and unwavering faith in the creative power of the mind, we sow the seeds of our desires and trust in the divine timing of their manifestation.

Embracing the Journey with Courage and Conviction

As we begin this journey of quantum visualisation, we are summoned to welcome it with bravery and confidence. Let go of doubts, fears, and limiting beliefs that may arise along the way, and instead, anchor yourself in a state of unwavering faith and trust. Trust in the inherent wisdom of the universe and the transformative power of your intentions. Trust in your ability to manifest your desires and create the life you envision.

A Call to Action

Today, I invite you to take a leap of faith and embrace the creative power of visualisation. Commit to a daily practice of visualisation with consistency, patience, and unwavering belief in your ability to manifest your desires. Trust in the process, stay open to the magic of the universe and watch as your dreams unfold before your eyes. Remember, you are the quantum creator of your reality, and with each visualisation, you are one step closer to realising your fullest potential and living the life of your dreams.

Chapter 4: Quantum Action

In this chapter, we'll define quantum action, the transformative power of intentional and aligned action inspired by the principles of quantum physics. The significance in the manifestation process, and discuss how taking action is essential for bringing manifestation goals into physical reality.

Understanding Quantum Action

Quantum action refers to intentional and aligned action taken with awareness and purpose, drawing inspiration from the principles of quantum physics. Just as thoughts and emotions influence our reality, so too does action play a crucial role in manifesting our desires. By taking deliberate and focused action that aligns with our intentions, we engage with the quantum field and co-create the reality we envision.

The Role of Action in Manifestation

Action is the bridge that connects our inner world of thoughts and intentions with the external world of physical reality. While visualisation and intention setting are powerful tools for manifestation, they must be accompanied by action to catalyse tangible results. Action transforms our dreams into tangible experiences, propelling us forward on the path toward our goals and aspirations.

Integrating Quantum Principles into Action

By integrating quantum principles into our actions, we align ourselves with the natural flow of the universe and amplify our manifestation efforts. Just as particles exhibit wave-like behaviour and respond to the observer's focus, so too do our actions carry energetic vibrations that influence the outcomes we experience. By infusing our actions with intention, mindfulness, and alignment with our goals, we tap into the quantum field of infinite potentiality and attract synchronicities and opportunities that support our journey.

Taking Inspired Action

Inspired action arises from a place of alignment with our deepest desires and inner guidance. It is an action that feels natural, effortless, and joyful, a reflection of our authentic selves and our true purpose. By following our intuition and inner wisdom, we discern which actions are in alignment with our goals and take deliberate steps toward their realisation.

Embracing the Journey

As we embark on the journey of quantum action, we embrace the inherent uncertainty and infinite possibilities that lie ahead. Each action we take is a step toward the manifestation of our desires, and each moment offers an opportunity for growth, learning, and expansion. With courage, intention, and a willingness to step into the unknown, we trust in the wisdom of the universe and the power of our actions to shape our reality. By aligning our actions with our intentions and infusing them with the energy of possibility, we harness the creative power of the universe and co-create the life of our dreams. We'll uncover how these two elements synergise, driving us closer to our desired outcomes, forming a powerful synergy that propels us toward our desired outcomes.

The Symbiotic Relationship

Visualisation and action are two essential components of the manifestation process, each playing a unique yet interconnected role in bringing our desires to fruition. Visualisation sets the stage for action by providing clarity, focus, and direction. When we visualise our goals with clarity and intention, we activate the creative power of our subconscious mind, aligning our thoughts and emotions with the desired outcome. This heightened state of awareness and alignment then prepares us to take inspired action in the physical world.

Clarifying Intentions Through Visualisation

Visualisation serves as a potent tool for clarifying our intentions and defining what we truly desire. By vividly imagining our goals as already achieved, we engage our subconscious mind and the quantum field, signalling our readiness to receive and manifest our desires. Visualisation cultivates a sense of certainty and conviction within us, reinforcing our belief in the possibility of achieving our goals.

As we immerse ourselves in the sensory experience of our desired outcomes, we program our subconscious mind to seek out opportunities and resources that support their realisation.

Focusing Attention on Desired Outcomes

Visualisation also plays a crucial role in focusing our attention on desired outcomes, guiding our thoughts and actions toward their attainment. When we consistently visualise our goals with clarity and emotion, we prime our subconscious mind to filter information and perceive opportunities that align with our intentions. This heightened state of awareness enables us to recognise synchronicities, serendipities, and inspired ideas that lead us closer to our desired outcomes. Visualisation acts as a beacon, illuminating the path ahead and empowering us to navigate challenges with resilience and determination.

Taking Inspired Action

While visualisation lays the foundation for manifestation, action is the catalyst that transforms our dreams into reality. Inspired action arises from a place of alignment with our intentions and inner guidance, propelling us toward our goals with clarity and purpose. When we combine visualisation with intentional action, we harness the full potential of the manifestation process, aligning our thoughts, emotions, and behaviours with our desired outcomes. Each action we take becomes imbued with the energy of possibility, moving us closer to the fulfilment of our dreams.

Embracing the Synergy

As we embrace the synergy between visualisation and action, we empower ourselves to manifest our desires with greater ease and efficiency. By integrating visualisation practices into our daily routines and taking inspired action toward our goals, we create a harmonious flow of energy that accelerates our manifestation efforts. With focused intention, unwavering belief, and consistent action, we become active participants in the co-creation of our reality, shaping our destiny with every thought, word, and deed.

By, exploring the profound implications of potentiality in quantum physics, we understand how we can leverage this concept to take inspired action in our lives. Searching the inherent possibilities that exist in the quantum realm, we unlock the keys to manifesting our deepest desires and transforming our reality.

Exploring the Quantum Landscape of Potentiality

At the heart of quantum physics lies the concept of potentiality, the idea that every conceivable outcome exists as a possibility until it is observed or collapsed into reality. Just as a wave function describes the range of possible states a particle can occupy, our lives are filled with endless possibilities waiting to be realised. By understanding the vast landscape of potentiality that surrounds us, we open ourselves to a world of infinite opportunities for growth, expansion, and manifestation.

Collapsing the Wave Function: The Role of Conscious Action

While potentiality offers us a glimpse into the boundless possibilities of the quantum realm, it is our conscious actions that serve as catalysts for collapsing the wave function and manifesting specific outcomes. Just as the act of observation influences the behaviour of particles in quantum mechanics, our focused attention and intention can shape the trajectory of our lives. By aligning our thoughts, beliefs, and actions with our desired outcomes, we harness the power of potentiality to bring our dreams into reality.

Embracing Quantum Flow: Effortless Action and Synchronicity

In the realm of quantum manifestation, action takes on a new meaning, one that is characterised by flow, synchronicity, and effortless manifestation. Rather than striving and struggling to force outcomes, we learn to surrender to the natural flow of the universe and allow synchronicities to guide our path. By tuning into the rhythm of the quantum field and following the breadcrumbs of inspiration, we effortlessly attract the people, resources, and opportunities needed to bring our visions to life.

Navigating the Quantum Landscape: Strategies for Inspired Action

Taking inspired action in alignment with our intentions requires a delicate balance of intuition, discernment, and trust. We will explore practical strategies for navigating the quantum landscape of potentiality and manifesting our desires with clarity and purpose. From setting clear intentions and visualising success to taking decisive steps toward our goals, we uncover the secrets to unlocking the full potential of our quantum reality.

Embodying the Quantum Creator: Becoming Agents of Change

As we conclude our exploration of quantum action, we are reminded of our inherent power as quantum creators of our reality. By embracing the concept of potentiality and taking inspired action in alignment with our intentions, we become agents of change capable of shaping our destiny and transforming our lives. With courage, intention, and unwavering faith in the infinite possibilities of the quantum universe, we step into our true power and manifest our wildest dreams with grace and ease.

As we delve into the crucial connection between intention and action in the process of quantum manifestation. By aligning our actions with our deepest intentions, we ensure coherence between our thoughts, beliefs, and behaviours, paving the way for the realisation of our desires.

Understanding the Power of Alignment

Alignment between intention and action is akin to tuning the strings of a finely crafted instrument. Just as a musician must tune each string to the correct frequency to produce harmonious music, so too must we align our actions with our intentions to create coherence in our lives. When our thoughts, beliefs, and behaviours are in harmony, we create a powerful resonance that amplifies our manifestation efforts and propels us toward our goals with clarity and purpose.

The Role of Inspired Action

Inspired action is action that arises from a place of alignment with our highest intentions and deepest desires. Unlike ordinary action, which may feel forced or disconnected from our true selves, inspired action flows effortlessly from a place of inner knowing and intuition. By cultivating a state of receptivity and attunement to the guidance of the quantum field, we can effortlessly discern the actions that are in alignment with our manifestation goals and take decisive steps toward their realisation.

Practical Strategies for Alignment

Aligning action with intention requires a conscious and deliberate approach to decision-making and behaviour. We explore practical strategies for identifying inspired actions and cultivating alignment in our daily lives. From mindfulness practices and intuitive listening to setting clear intentions and following our heart's guidance, we uncover the keys to unlocking the power of aligned action and manifesting our desires with greater ease and efficiency.

Overcoming Resistance and Obstacles

Despite our best intentions, we may encounter resistance and obstacles along the path of aligned action. Whether it be self-doubt, fear of failure, or external challenges, these obstacles can derail our progress and undermine our manifestation efforts. Here, we confront these challenges head-on and explore strategies for overcoming resistance and staying aligned with our intentions. By cultivating resilience, perseverance, and a willingness to adapt, we can navigate the twists and turns of our journey with grace and confidence.

Embodying the Quantum Creator

As we integrate the principles of alignment and inspired action into our lives, we step into our role as quantum creators of our reality. By aligning our thoughts, beliefs, and behaviours with our deepest intentions, we harness the power of the quantum field to manifest our desires and create the life of our dreams. With each aligned action we take, we affirm our commitment to living in harmony with the universe and embodying the infinite potential that resides within us.

While we investigate the dynamic interplay between inspired action, flow, and synchronicity in the journey of quantum manifestation. By aligning with the natural rhythm of the universe and cultivating a state of flow, we open ourselves to serendipitous encounters, favourable circumstances, and meaningful connections that effortlessly propel us toward our goals.

Understanding the Flow State

The flow state, often described as a state of effortless concentration and peak performance, is characterised by a deep sense of immersion and engagement in an activity. When we are in flow, time seems to fade away, and our actions unfold with seamless precision and ease. By tapping into the flow state, we unlock our full creative potential and experience a profound sense of fulfilment and joy in our endeavours.

Cultivating Flow through Inspired Action

Inspired action serves as the gateway to the flow state, guiding us toward activities and pursuits that resonate with our deepest intentions and desires. When we take inspired action, we align ourselves with the natural flow of the universe, allowing opportunities to effortlessly present themselves and synchronicities to unfold in our lives. By following our intuition and listening to the subtle whispers of the quantum field, we navigate our journey with grace and ease, guided by the currents of divine inspiration.

Embracing Synchronicity as a Signpost

Synchronicity, often described as meaningful coincidences or serendipitous encounters, serves as a guiding force on our path of quantum manifestation. When we are in alignment with our intentions and attuned to the flow of the universe, synchronicities abound, leading us toward our goals with precision and clarity. By recognising and embracing these synchronicities as signposts from the universe, we deepen our trust in the inherent wisdom of the quantum field and open ourselves to the infinite possibilities that lie ahead.

Navigating the River of Life

Life is like a flowing river, constantly evolving and unfolding in unpredictable ways. By embracing the flow of life and surrendering to its currents, we release the need for control and allow ourselves to be carried effortlessly toward our destiny.

Riding the Waves of Quantum Manifestation

As we conclude our exploration of flow and synchronicity in the context of quantum manifestation, we are reminded of the inherent beauty and wisdom of the universe. By aligning with the flow of the quantum stream and embracing the synchronicities that abound, we unlock the full potential of our creative power and manifest our desires with grace and ease.

While addressing the significant hurdles that often impede us from taking inspired action on our journey of quantum manifestation, we can transcend fear, self-doubt, and inertia by comprehending the nature of resistance and equipping ourselves with effective strategies. This enables us to embrace our full potential and confidently enter the flow of creation.

Understanding the Nature of Resistance

Resistance manifests in myriad forms, from the subtle whispers of self-doubt to the paralysing grip of fear. At its core, resistance is the voice of the ego, seeking to keep us safe within the confines of our comfort zone. By recognising resistance as a natural part of the creative process, we can begin to disarm its power and move forward with courage and conviction.

Identifying Common Obstacles

Fear, self-doubt, and inertia are among the most common obstacles we encounter on the path of inspired action. Fear of failure, rejection, or judgment can immobilise us, preventing us from taking the risks necessary for growth and expansion. Self-doubt whispers insidious lies, eroding our confidence and undermining our belief in ourselves. Inertia keeps us stuck in familiar patterns and resistant to change and growth.

Strategies for Overcoming Resistance

To overcome resistance, we must first shine a light on the shadows that lurk in the recesses of our minds. By bringing awareness to our fears, doubts, and limiting beliefs, we can begin to challenge their validity and reclaim our power. Affirmations, visualisation, and positive self-talk are powerful tools for reprogramming the subconscious mind and cultivating a mindset of resilience and confidence.

Stepping into Courageous Action

Taking inspired action requires courage, the willingness to face our fears and move forward despite them. From setting clear intentions and breaking tasks down into manageable steps to seeking support from mentors and accountability partners, we empower ourselves to overcome resistance and embrace our highest potential.

Embracing the Journey of Growth

As we navigate the twists and turns of the creative process, we are reminded that growth often lies on the other side of resistance. By embracing challenges as opportunities for learning and expansion, we transform obstacles into stepping stones on our path of evolution. With each courageous step we take, we move closer to realising our dreams and embodying the fullest expression of our true selves.

The Triumph of the Human Spirit

Overcoming resistance is not merely a task to be accomplished but a testament to the indomitable spirit of the human heart. As we face our fears, conquer our doubts, and take bold and decisive action, we unleash the infinite potential that lies within us and step into our role as conscious creators of our reality.

The profound impact of momentum on the manifestation process, illuminating how consistent and aligned action can harness the power of quantum physics will propel us toward our goals with unstoppable force. By understanding the dynamics of momentum and learning to harness its transformative potential, we unlock the key to exponential progress and manifestation success.

Understanding the Nature of Momentum

Momentum is the force that drives us forward on our journey of manifestation, amplifying our efforts and propelling us toward our desired outcomes. Like a snowball rolling downhill, momentum builds upon itself, gaining speed and power with each successive action. By taking consistent and aligned action, we set the wheels of manifestation in motion, creating a powerful force that cannot be easily stopped or redirected.

Harnessing the Power of Quantum Momentum

In the realm of quantum physics, momentum is not merely a physical phenomenon but a fundamental aspect of the fabric of reality itself. Just as particles in motion tend to stay in motion, so too do our thoughts, beliefs, and actions create ripples of energy that shape the course of our lives. By aligning our actions with our intentions and maintaining a steady focus on our goals, we tap into the inherent power of quantum momentum to manifest our desires with greater speed and efficiency.

Cultivating Consistency and Alignment

Consistency and alignment are the twin pillars upon which quantum momentum is built. Consistency involves showing up day after day, regardless of external circumstances, and taking deliberate action toward our goals. Alignment, on the other hand, requires us to ensure that our actions are in harmony with our intentions and values, avoiding distractions and detours that may derail our progress. By cultivating both consistency and alignment in our lives, we create a fertile ground for quantum momentum to flourish.

Breaking Through Resistance and Obstacles

Despite our best efforts, resistance and obstacles may arise along the path of momentum, threatening to slow our progress or divert us from our chosen course. Ongoing, we explore strategies for overcoming resistance and breaking through obstacles, including mindset shifts, accountability structures, and self-care practices. By facing our challenges with courage and resilience, we transform obstacles into opportunities for growth and expansion, further fuelling the momentum of manifestation.

Celebrating Progress and Success

As we harness the power of quantum momentum to propel us toward our goals, it's important to pause along the way to celebrate our progress and successes. Each milestone achieved is a testament to our dedication and determination, reminding us of the infinite potential that lies within us. By acknowledging and honouring our achievements, we reinforce our belief in ourselves and our ability to create the life of our dreams.

The Momentum of Manifestation

Quantum momentum is the engine that drives the manifestation process forward, accelerating our progress and amplifying our results. By embracing consistency, alignment, and resilience, we tap into the limitless power of the quantum universe to manifest our desires with grace and ease.

In this part, we examine practical strategies for smoothly incorporating inspired action into our daily routines, cultivating a culture of consistency, momentum, and progress in our manifestation journey. By giving priority to our goals, refining our routines, and infusing purpose into every moment, we establish the groundwork for continuous growth and transformation.

The Power of Daily Practice

Daily practice forms the bedrock of our manifestation journey, providing a structured framework within which we can consistently take intentional steps toward our goals. Whether through morning rituals, evening reflections, or midday check-ins, daily practice serves as a constant reminder of our commitment to our vision and keeps us anchored in the present moment.

Setting Clear Goals and Intentions

Central to integrating action into daily practice is the clarity of our goals and intentions. By defining our objectives with precision and specificity, we provide ourselves with a roadmap for action and create a clear path toward manifestation success. Whether short-term or long-term, personal or professional, our goals serve as beacons guiding our actions and decisions each day.

Prioritising Tasks and Activities

In a world filled with distractions and competing demands, prioritisation is key to ensuring that our actions are aligned with our highest priorities and values. By identifying the most important tasks and activities that contribute to our goals, we can allocate our time and energy effectively, maximising our impact and progress toward manifestation.

Creating Rituals and Routines

Rituals and routines serve as the scaffolding upon which we build our daily practice, providing structure, consistency, and predictability to our actions. Whether through morning rituals that set the tone for the day ahead or evening routines that facilitate reflection and integration, these practices help us stay grounded and focused amidst the chaos of daily life.

Infusing Every Moment with Purpose

Beyond formal rituals and routines, integrating action into daily practice involves infusing every moment with purpose and intentionality. From mundane tasks to significant milestones, every action we take is an opportunity to align with our goals, values, and aspirations, moving us closer to the life we envision for ourselves.

Staying Flexible and Adaptable

While routines and rituals provide stability and structure, it's essential to remain flexible and adaptable in our approach to daily practice. Life is unpredictable, and circumstances may change unexpectedly, requiring us to pivot, adjust, and recalibrate our actions accordingly. By embracing change and uncertainty, we cultivate resilience and agility in the face of adversity, ensuring that our momentum toward manifestation remains unshakeable.

The Art of Daily Manifestation

In conclusion, integrating action into daily practice is the art of turning our intentions into reality, one step at a time. By setting clear goals, prioritising tasks, and infusing every moment with purpose, we harness the power of consistency and momentum to manifest our desires with greater speed and efficiency.

Next, we look into the dynamic intersection of quantum action and personal/professional growth, illuminating how intentional and aligned action can catalyse transformative change across all aspects of our lives. By harnessing the principles of quantum physics, we unlock new pathways for advancement, development, and fulfilment, realising our fullest potential in both our personal and professional spheres.

The Quantum Approach to Achievement

At the heart of quantum action lies a fundamental shift in our approach to achievement, one that transcends traditional notions of effort and struggle and embraces the flow of inspired action. Rather than striving to force outcomes through sheer willpower, we learn to trust in the inherent intelligence of the universe and collaborate with its unfolding, co-creating our reality with intentionality and purpose.

Career Advancement through Quantum Action

In the realm of professional growth, quantum action empowers us to take bold and strategic steps toward our career aspirations, whether it's pursuing new opportunities, expanding our skill set, or cultivating influential connections. By aligning our actions with our professional goals and vision, we position ourselves as active agents of change in our careers, driving innovation, progress, and success.

Personal Development and Quantum Leaps

In the realm of personal development, quantum action catalyses profound transformation and evolution, enabling us to break free from limiting patterns, expand our consciousness, and actualise our highest potential. From adopting empowering beliefs to embracing discomfort as a catalyst for growth, every action we take becomes an opportunity for self-discovery, empowerment, and liberation.

Relationships and Quantum Connection

In the realm of relationships, quantum action fosters deeper connections, mutual understanding, and harmony, enriching our interactions with authenticity, empathy, and presence. By approaching our relationships with intentionality and mindfulness, we cultivate environments of trust, respect, and support, nurturing bonds that uplift and inspire us on our journey of personal and collective growth.

Real-Life Examples and Success Stories

Throughout these pages, we draw inspiration from real-life examples and success stories that illustrate the transformative power of quantum action in action. From individuals who have manifested their dream careers to couples who have revitalised their relationships through intentional communication and presence, these stories serve as beacons of possibility, reminding us of the boundless potential that lies within each of us.

These real-life examples demonstrate how quantum action can lead to transformative outcomes in various areas of life, from career fulfilment and relationship revitalisation to health and wellness transformation and financial abundance. By harnessing the power of intention, belief, and aligned action, individuals can manifest their dreams and unlock their full potential.

Career Manifestation: Sarah is a graphic designer who dreamed of starting her own design agency but felt overwhelmed by self-doubt and fear of failure. Through the practice of quantum action, she began taking small, intentional steps toward her goal, such as updating her portfolio, networking with industry professionals, and attending entrepreneurship workshops. Over time, her confidence grew, and she attracted opportunities to collaborate with like-minded creatives. Today, Sarah's design agency is thriving, and she credits her success to the power of taking aligned action towards her dreams.

Relationship Revitalisation: Mark and Emily had been married for ten years but felt disconnected and unhappy in their relationship. They decided to embark on a journey of intentional communication and presence, inspired by the principles of quantum action. Instead

of allowing their past grievances to dictate their interactions, they focused on expressing gratitude, listening actively, and nurturing their connection in the present moment. Through consistent effort and vulnerability, Mark and Emily rediscovered the love and passion that initially brought them together, revitalising their marriage and deepening their bond.

Health and Wellness Transformation: James struggled with chronic health issues and felt trapped in a cycle of pain and frustration. Determined to reclaim his vitality, he adopted a holistic approach to healing that combined quantum action with lifestyle changes such as regular exercise, nutritious diet, and mindfulness practices. By committing to his well-being and taking empowered action towards his health goals, James experienced significant improvements in his physical and mental health. Today, he leads an active and fulfilling life, free from the limitations that once held him back.

Creative Fulfilment: Emma always had a passion for writing but struggled to find the courage to pursue her dream of becoming a published author. With the support of quantum action principles, she committed to writing every day, setting aside self-doubt and perfectionism. Through consistent effort and dedication, Emma completed her first novel and secured a publishing deal with a renowned literary agent. Her story serves as a reminder that by aligning our actions with our aspirations, we can bring our creative visions to life and share them with the world.

Financial Abundance: Jason had always lived paycheque to paycheque and felt stuck in a cycle of scarcity. Inspired by the concept of quantum action, he decided to shift his mindset from lack to abundance and take proactive steps to improve his financial situation. Jason enrolled in financial literacy courses, created a budgeting plan, and explored new income streams such as freelance work and investing. Through disciplined action and a belief in his ability to attract abundance, Jason experienced a dramatic increase in his income and achieved financial freedom.

Embracing Quantum Action

Quantum action is not merely a strategy for achievement but a way of being a profound shift in consciousness that empowers us to live with purpose, passion, and presence. As we continue to apply the principles of quantum physics to our personal and professional lives, may we embrace the limitless possibilities that unfold before us, trusting in our ability to create the reality we desire and deserve.

As we unearth the transformative potential of quantum action, illuminating its role as a catalyst for personal growth, manifestation, and fulfilment. Through reflection, insight, and practical guidance, we embrace the power of intentional and aligned action, recognising it as the driving force behind the realisation of our deepest desires and aspirations.

The Quantum Leap: From Potential to Reality

At the heart of quantum action lies the concept of the quantum leap, a profound shift in consciousness and behaviour that propels us from the realm of possibility to the realm of actuality. By embracing the quantum leap mindset, we transcend self-imposed limitations and boldly step into the unknown, trusting in our innate ability to co-create our reality with the universe.

From Intention to Action: Bridging the Gap

Purpose without action remains merely a desire, yet when paired with intentional and decisive action, it transforms into a powerful catalyst for manifestation. We investigate the dynamic relationship between intention and action, emphasising the significance of closing the divide between vision and implementation to materialise our aspirations into concrete reality.

Embracing the Unknown: Cultivating a Fearless Mindset

One of the greatest barriers to quantum action is the fear of the unknown, the uncertainty and discomfort that accompany stepping outside our comfort zones. Yet, it is precisely in the realm of the unknown that true growth and transformation occur. Through introspection and reflection, we learn to embrace uncertainty as a catalyst for expansion, courageously venturing into uncharted territory with curiosity and resilience.

Confidence in Action: Trusting the Process

To fully harness the power of quantum action, we must cultivate unwavering confidence in our ability to manifest our desires and navigate the twists and turns of the journey ahead. By trusting in the process and believing in our innate potential, we fortify our resolve and open ourselves to the abundance of possibilities that await us on the path to self-realisation.

The Ripple Effect: Impact Beyond the Individual

As we embrace quantum action in our own lives, we become agents of transformation not only for ourselves but also for the world around us. Our actions send ripples of influence into the collective consciousness, inspiring others to embark on their journeys of growth and empowerment.

Conclusion: Embracing Quantum Action

In conclusion, the power of quantum action lies not only in its ability to manifest our desires but also in its capacity to catalyse collective change and usher in a new paradigm of possibility and potential. As we embark on this journey of self-discovery and manifestation, may we embrace the transformative potential of quantum action with open hearts and courageous spirits, knowing that with each step we take, we draw closer to the realisation of our deepest dreams and aspirations.

Chapter 5: Quantum Resilience

In this chapter, we initiate an exploration into the domain of quantum resilience, a profound and transformative method for navigating life's challenges with grace, fortitude, and unwavering determination. We examine the core of resilience through the perspective of quantum physics, shedding light on its ability to stimulate personal growth, nurture inner strength, and cultivate a deep sense of well-being.

Defining Quantum Resilience: Adapting to the Flux of Life

Quantum resilience is more than just bouncing back from setbacks; it is about embracing the inherent fluidity and uncertainty of existence, recognising that change is the only constant in the universe. We define quantum resilience as the ability to adapt and thrive in the face of adversity, drawing inspiration from the dynamic nature of quantum phenomena to inform our understanding of resilience in the human experience.

The Quantum Mindset: Shifting Perspectives on Resilience

At the heart of quantum resilience lies a fundamental shift in mindset, a willingness to embrace change, uncertainty, and discomfort as catalysts for growth and transformation. By adopting a quantum mindset, we reframe adversity as an opportunity for learning and evolution, empowering ourselves to navigate life's challenges with courage and resilience.

The Power of Quantum Adaptation: Embracing Change with Grace

In the ever-changing landscape of existence, the ability to adapt is essential for survival and flourishing. We will explore how quantum principles such as superposition and entanglement can inform our approach to adaptation, highlighting the importance of flexibility, openness, and resilience in the face of adversity.

Harnessing Quantum Resources: Cultivating Inner Strength and Resilience

Just as particles draw upon quantum fields of energy to manifest their reality, we access internal wellsprings of resilience, wisdom, and strength to gracefully confront life's trials. Through mindfulness practices, self-care rituals, and spiritual nourishment, we cultivate the inner resources needed to weather the storms of life and emerge stronger and more resilient than ever before.

The Quantum Ripple Effect: Spreading Resilience Through Connection

As we cultivate quantum resilience in our own lives, we become beacons of light and inspiration for others, illuminating the path to resilience and empowerment through our example. We explore the ripple effect of quantum resilience, celebrating its power to uplift and transform not only ourselves but also the world around us.

Embracing the Quantum Resilience Journey

Quantum resilience invites us to embrace life's challenges with courage, resilience, and an unwavering belief in our innate capacity to thrive amidst adversity. As we embark on this journey of self-discovery and empowerment, may we draw strength from the wisdom of quantum physics, trusting in the boundless potential of the human spirit to overcome obstacles, transcend limitations, and manifest our highest aspirations.

Into the nature of adversity, a fundamental aspect of the human experience that shapes our journey of personal growth and self-discovery. Through the lens of quantum manifestation, we explore the transformative power of adversity, illuminating its role as a catalyst for growth, resilience, and profound inner transformation.

Understanding Adversity: The Crucible of Personal Evolution

Adversity is an inherent part of life, an inevitable byproduct of our journey through the ever-changing landscape of existence. We examine the multifaceted nature of adversity, exploring its myriad forms and manifestations, from personal setbacks and challenges to global crises and upheavals. We acknowledge the discomfort and uncertainty that adversity brings while recognising its potential to catalyse profound shifts in consciousness and behaviour.

Embracing the Gift of Adversity: Lessons in Resilience and Self-Discovery

Contrary to popular belief, adversity is not merely an obstacle to be overcome; it is a teacher, guiding us along the path of self-discovery and personal evolution. Here, we investigate the transformative potential of adversity, highlighting how challenges provide opportunities for learning, growth, and resilience. We look into the invaluable lessons that adversity teaches us about ourselves, our values, and our priorities, inviting us to embrace each obstacle as a stepping stone on the path to self-realisation.

The Quantum Perspective on Adversity: Embracing Change and Uncertainty

From a quantum perspective, adversity is not something to be feared or resisted but embraced as an integral part of the creative process. We draw upon the principles of quantum physics to illuminate the nature of adversity, highlighting its inherent connection to change, uncertainty, and the flux of existence. We look at how the dynamic interplay of energy and consciousness shapes our experience of adversity, inviting us to embrace change with courage, resilience, and an unwavering trust in the wisdom of the universe.

Transforming Adversity into Opportunity: Cultivating Quantum Resilience

As we navigate the challenges of life, we have the power to transform adversity into opportunity, drawing upon our inner reserves of strength, resilience, and wisdom. We will explore practical strategies for cultivating quantum resilience in the face of adversity, from mindfulness practices and self-care rituals to cognitive reframing techniques and spiritual nourishment. We celebrate the transformative potential of adversity, recognising it as a catalyst for growth, empowerment, and the realisation of our highest potential.

Embracing the Journey of Adversity and Growth

Adversity is not the enemy but a faithful companion on the journey of self-discovery and personal evolution. As we embrace the challenges that life presents us with, may we cultivate a spirit of resilience, courage, and open-heartedness, knowing that each obstacle we encounter is an opportunity for growth, transformation, and the manifestation of our deepest desires.

Exploring the concept of quantum adaptation, is an essential aspect of quantum resilience that empowers us to navigate life's ever-changing landscape with grace, flexibility, and resilience. Drawing inspiration from the dynamic nature of particles in the quantum realm, we look into how the principles of adaptation can inform our approach to personal growth, transformation, and the manifestation of our desires.

Understanding Quantum Adaptation: Embracing Change as a Catalyst for Growth

Adaptation is a fundamental aspect of life, a dynamic process that allows organisms to respond and adjust to changes in their environment. We examine the concept of adaptation through the lens of quantum physics, highlighting how particles in the quantum realm exhibit remarkable flexibility and resilience in the face of shifting conditions. We look at how the parallels between quantum adaptation and our capacity to evolve and transform in response to life's challenges, inviting us to embrace change as a catalyst for growth and self-discovery.

The Quantum Dance of Change: Embracing Flux and Uncertainty

Change is the only constant in the universe, a dynamic dance of energy and consciousness that shapes the fabric of reality. Examining the nature of change from a quantum perspective highlights its intrinsic connection to uncertainty, flux, and infinite possibility. Inviting us to embrace change with curiosity, openness, and an unwavering trust in the inherent wisdom of the universe, the principles of quantum physics illuminate the fluid nature of existence.

Adapting to the Flow of Life: Strategies for Quantum Resilience

As we navigate the ebb and flow of life, we have the opportunity to cultivate quantum resilience, an inner resource that enables us to adapt and thrive in the face of adversity.

Showing the practical strategies for cultivating quantum adaptation, from mindfulness practices and emotional intelligence to flexibility, creativity, and a willingness to let go of attachments. We celebrate the transformative potential of adaptation, recognising it as a pathway to greater freedom, resilience, and fulfilment.

Harnessing the Power of Quantum Adaptation: Manifesting Our Deepest Desires

Ultimately, quantum adaptation empowers us to manifest our deepest desires by aligning with the dynamic flow of the universe and responding with flexibility and resilience to life's challenges. Exploring how cultivating a mindset of adaptation can enhance our manifestation efforts, allowing us to navigate obstacles with grace and confidence. Trust in the inherent intelligence of the quantum universe to guide us on our journey of self-discovery and personal evolution.

We now embark on a journey to cultivate inner strength, an essential component of quantum resilience that empowers us to navigate life's challenges with grace, courage, and resilience. We explore practical strategies grounded in mindfulness, self-care, and mindset shifts, inviting you to harness your inner resources and tap into the limitless potential of the quantum realm.

The Power of Inner Strength:

Inner strength is not merely about physical prowess or endurance but encompasses a deep reservoir of resilience, courage, and fortitude that resides within each of us.

Mindfulness Practices for Resilience:

Mindfulness is a powerful tool for cultivating inner strength, allowing us to cultivate present-moment awareness, regulate our emotions, and cultivate a sense of calm amidst life's storms. Within this segment, we look into mindfulness practices such as meditation, breathwork, and body scans, offering practical techniques for fostering resilience and emotional well-being.

Meet Alex, a busy professional juggling a demanding job and family responsibilities. Despite his hectic schedule, Alex noticed that stress and anxiety were starting to take a toll on his mental and emotional well-being. Determined to find a way to cope, Alex turned to mindfulness practices as a tool for managing his stress and building resilience.

First, Alex began incorporating mindfulness meditation into his daily routine. Each morning, he set aside ten minutes to sit quietly and focus on his breath, allowing thoughts to come and go without judgment. Through regular meditation practice, Alex learned to cultivate a sense of calm and inner peace, even in the midst of chaos.

In addition to meditation, Alex practiced breathwork techniques to help regulate his emotions and reduce stress. During moments of tension or overwhelm, Alex would take slow, deep breaths, focusing on the sensation of air entering and leaving his body. This simple yet powerful practice allowed him to centre himself and respond to challenges with greater clarity and composure.

Finally, Alex explored body scan meditations as a way to release physical tension and cultivate awareness of his body's sensations. Using guided audio recordings, Alex would systematically scan his body from head to toe, noticing areas of tension and gently releasing any tightness or discomfort. This practice not only helped Alex relax his body but also deepened his connection to himself and his inner resources.

Over time, Alex noticed significant improvements in his resilience and emotional well-being. By incorporating mindfulness practices into his daily life, he learned to navigate stress with greater ease and respond to challenges with a sense of equanimity. Through mindfulness, Alex discovered a powerful tool for building resilience and fostering emotional well-being in the face of life's inevitable ups and downs.

As we discuss mindfulness practices within this segment, let Alex's journey inspire us to explore these techniques for ourselves, discovering their transformative potential for fostering resilience and emotional well-being in our own lives.

Self-Care as a Path to Resilience:

Self-care is an essential aspect of nurturing inner strength, providing us with the energy and vitality needed to face life's challenges with grace and resilience. We seek the importance of self-care routines tailored to individual needs, from physical exercise and nourishing nutrition to restorative practices such as journaling, creative expression, and spending time in nature.

Harnessing the Power of Positive Psychology:

Positive psychology offers valuable insights into cultivating inner strength and resilience, emphasising the importance of cultivating a positive mindset, fostering gratitude, and cultivating resilience in the face of adversity. Practical strategies for shifting perspective, reframing challenges as opportunities for growth, and cultivating a resilient mindset grounded in optimism and hope are discussed.

Building Resilient Mindsets:

Our mindset plays a crucial role in shaping our experience of adversity, influencing how we interpret challenges and respond to setbacks. The concept of a growth mindset, a belief in our ability to learn, grow, and adapt, is discussed, along with practical strategies for cultivating resilience in the face of adversity, such as reframing negative self-talk, embracing failure as a learning opportunity, and fostering self-compassion.

Embracing Adversity as a Catalyst for Growth:

Adversity is not merely a test of our strength but can also serve as a catalyst for growth, offering valuable lessons and opportunities for self-discovery. The transformative potential of adversity is discussed, inviting you to embrace challenges with an open heart and a willingness to learn, grow, and evolve.

Understanding Change Through a Quantum Lens:

Change is an inherent aspect of the quantum realm, where particles constantly shift and transform in response to shifting conditions. Quantum principles such as superposition and entanglement offer insights into the fluid and dynamic nature of reality, challenging us to embrace change as an opportunity for growth and transformation rather than a source of fear or resistance.

The Power of Flexibility and Adaptability:

Flexibility and adaptability are essential qualities for navigating the ever-changing landscape of life. We see how cultivating these qualities can help us respond effectively to unexpected challenges, seize growth opportunities, and thrive in times of uncertainty. Drawing inspiration from quantum physics, we learn to take on change with a sense of curiosity and openness, trusting in the inherent wisdom of the universe.

Embracing Uncertainty as a Catalyst for Growth:

Uncertainty can be unsettling, but it also holds the potential for profound growth and transformation. How quantum principles, such as the uncertainty principle, encourage us to embrace uncertainty as a natural and unavoidable aspect of life is examined. Navigating uncertainty with courage and resilience can lead to new insights, experiences, and opportunities, ultimately enriching our journey of self-discovery and personal evolution.

Cultivating Resilience in the Face of Change:

Resilience is the ability to adapt and thrive in the face of adversity, uncertainty, and change. We will delve into practical strategies for cultivating resilience, drawing inspiration from quantum principles such as quantum adaptation and quantum resilience. Through mindfulness practices, positive psychology techniques, and mindset shifts, we learn to navigate change with grace and resilience, trusting in our inner strength and resilience to carry us through life's challenges.

Meet Maya, a young professional navigating the ups and downs of a competitive job market. Despite her best efforts, Maya faced rejection after rejection in her job search, leading to feelings of frustration and self-doubt. Determined to bounce back stronger, Maya turned to mindfulness practices, positive psychology techniques, and mindset shifts to cultivate resilience in the face of uncertainty.

First, Maya began incorporating mindfulness meditation into her daily routine. Each morning, she set aside time to sit quietly and observe her thoughts and emotions without judgment. Through mindfulness practice, Maya learned to cultivate a sense of inner calm and presence, allowing her to respond to challenges with greater clarity and perspective.

In addition to mindfulness, Maya embraced positive psychology techniques to foster a more resilient mindset. She started practicing gratitude journaling, taking time each day to reflect on the things she was grateful for in her life. By focusing on the positive aspects of her experience, Maya was able to reframe setbacks as opportunities for growth and learning.

Finally, Maya adopted mindset shifts inspired by quantum principles such as quantum adaptation and resilience. She recognised that change was inevitable and that she had the power to adapt and thrive in any situation. Instead of seeing rejection as a personal failure, Maya viewed it as a stepping stone on her journey to success, trusting in her inner strength and resilience to carry her through life's challenges.

Over time, Maya noticed a significant improvement in her ability to bounce back from adversity. By cultivating resilience through mindfulness, positive psychology, and quantum-inspired mindset shifts, Maya learned to navigate change with grace and confidence, trusting in her ability to overcome any obstacle that came her way.

Embracing Change as a Path to Personal Evolution:

Change is not merely an external force but also a catalyst for personal evolution and growth. We will show how embracing change can lead to greater self-awareness, self-discovery, and self-transformation. By releasing resistance and embracing the flow of life, we open ourselves to new possibilities, opportunities, and experiences, ultimately expanding our consciousness and deepening our connection to the quantum fabric of reality.

By embracing change as a natural and inevitable aspect of life, we can cultivate flexibility, resilience, and adaptability, empowering ourselves to navigate life's challenges with grace and confidence. In doing so, we align ourselves with the dynamic and transformative energy of the quantum realm, embracing change as a powerful catalyst for self-discovery, personal evolution, and manifesting our deepest desires.

Understanding the Quantum Growth Mindset:

The quantum growth mindset is a perspective rooted in quantum principles that recognises the inherent potential for growth and transformation in every experience. Showing how adopting a quantum growth mindset involves embracing uncertainty, reframing challenges as opportunities for learning, and cultivating resilience in the face of adversity. Drawing inspiration from quantum physics, we learn to view setbacks as stepping stones to success and setbacks as opportunities for growth.

Embracing the Power of Perception:

Perception plays a crucial role in shaping our experiences and responses to challenges. We examine how adopting a quantum growth mindset involves shifting our perception of challenges from threats to opportunities. By reframing challenges as opportunities for growth and learning, we empower ourselves to approach obstacles with curiosity, openness, and optimism, ultimately unlocking our full potential for personal development and self-mastery.

Cultivating Resilience in the Face of Adversity:

Resilience is the ability to adapt and thrive in the face of adversity, setbacks, and challenges., explaining practical strategies for cultivating resilience through the lens of the quantum growth mindset. By embracing challenges as opportunities for growth, practicing self-compassion, and fostering a sense of purpose and meaning, we empower ourselves to navigate life's ups and downs with grace and resilience, ultimately emerging stronger and more resilient than before.

Transforming Obstacles into Opportunities:

Obstacles are not roadblocks but rather opportunities for growth and learning, showing how adopting a quantum growth mindset involves reframing obstacles as opportunities for creativity, innovation, and personal development. By embracing the uncertainty and complexity of life, we open ourselves to new possibilities, perspectives, and experiences, ultimately unleashing our full potential for growth, success, and fulfilment.

Embracing Lifelong Learning and Growth:

Learning is a lifelong journey of exploration, discovery, and growth, exploring how adopting a quantum growth mindset involves embracing lifelong learning and personal development. By cultivating a sense of curiosity, openness, and wonder, we invite new experiences, insights, and opportunities into our lives, ultimately expanding our consciousness and deepening our connection to the quantum fabric of reality.

By reframing challenges as opportunities for growth, cultivating resilience in the face of adversity, and embracing lifelong learning and personal development, we empower ourselves to navigate life's ups and downs with grace, courage, and resilience. In doing so, we align ourselves with the dynamic and transformative energy of the quantum realm, unlocking our full potential for growth, success, and self-mastery.

Understanding Quantum Healing:

Quantum healing is a holistic approach to healing that recognises the interconnectedness of body, mind, and spirit. Following on, we examine how quantum resilience facilitates healing by restoring balance and harmony across dimensions.

Drawing from quantum physics, we explore the concept of the quantum field as a vast, interconnected matrix of energy and information that underlies all existence, and how practices such as energy healing, visualisation, and self-reflection can tap into this field to promote healing and transformation.

Healing on the Physical Level:

The physical body is a dynamic and interconnected system that is constantly seeking balance and harmony. We explore how quantum resilience supports healing on the physical level by addressing the root causes of illness and imbalance. We will look into practices such as energy healing, sound therapy, and body awareness techniques that promote relaxation, vitality, and cellular rejuvenation, ultimately fostering a state of optimal health and well-being.

Healing on the Emotional Level:

Emotions are powerful messengers that provide valuable insights into our inner world and guide us toward greater wholeness and integration. We look at how quantum resilience supports healing on the emotional level by facilitating the release of emotional blockages and traumas. We explore practices such as mindfulness, emotional processing, and inner child work that promote emotional awareness, resilience, and self-compassion, ultimately fostering a sense of emotional balance and inner peace.

Healing on the Spiritual Level:

Spiritual healing is a journey of self-discovery, self-realisation, and alignment with our highest potential. We see how quantum resilience supports healing on the spiritual level by facilitating connection with our inner wisdom and higher guidance. Practices such as meditation, visualisation, and soul retrieval that promote spiritual growth, expansion, and enlightenment, ultimately fosters a sense of wholeness and connection to the divine.

Transformation and Integration:

Transformation is a natural process of growth and evolution that unfolds as we journey through life, and how quantum resilience supports transformation by facilitating the integration of healing experiences and insights into our daily lives. Practices such as journaling, creative expression, and rituals that promote self-reflection, integration, and alignment with our true essence, ultimately fosters a sense of wholeness and empowerment.

By nurturing wholeness and vitality on physical, emotional, and spiritual levels, we empower ourselves to embody our fullest potential and create a life of joy, fulfilment, and abundance. In doing so, we align ourselves with the dynamic and transformative energy of the quantum realm, unlocking our innate capacity for healing, growth, and self-realisation.

As we embark on a journey of self-discovery and empowerment, we explore the transformative process of overcoming limiting beliefs and patterns. We investigate the profound impact that our beliefs and thought patterns have on our resilience and personal growth, and we uncover practical strategies for breaking free from the shackles of self-imposed limitations to unlock our quantum potential.

Understanding Limiting Beliefs and Patterns:

Limiting beliefs and patterns are like invisible chains that hold us back from reaching our full potential. Imagine Amy, a talented artist with a passion for painting, but she's always felt insecure about her work. Amy's limiting belief is that she's not good enough, stemming from past experiences of criticism and self-doubt.

Throughout her childhood, Amy's artistic endeavours were met with scepticism from her family and teachers, who encouraged her to pursue more practical career paths. Over time, Amy internalised these messages, forming a belief that her art was not valuable or worthy of recognition.

As Amy grew older, she continued to encounter situations that reinforced her limiting belief. Rejections from art galleries, comparisons to other artists, and her own harsh self-criticism all served to validate her belief that she was not good enough.

These limiting beliefs manifested in Amy's life as self-sabotaging behaviours and a fear of taking risks. She avoided submitting her work for exhibitions, hesitated to pursue opportunities for growth, and constantly doubted her abilities as an artist.

Looking into how limiting beliefs and patterns are formed through past experiences, societal conditioning, and self-perception, we explore the impact of these beliefs on our thoughts, behaviours, and emotions, recognising how they hold us back from embracing change, taking risks, and pursuing our dreams.

Identifying Limiting Beliefs and Patterns:

Acknowledgment is the first step towards transformation. Practical techniques for identifying limiting beliefs and patterns that may impede our resilience and personal growth. We examine the importance of self-reflection, journaling, and mindfulness in uncovering hidden beliefs and patterns, allowing us to bring to light the subconscious programming that influences our thoughts, emotions, and behaviors.

Reframing Negative Thought Patterns:

Once we've identified our limiting beliefs and patterns, the next step is to reframe them into empowering narratives that support our growth and evolution. We explore the power of cognitive reframing techniques such as positive affirmations, visualisation, and gratitude practices. We discuss how these techniques can help us challenge negative thought patterns, shift our perspective, and cultivate a mindset of abundance, resilience, and possibility.

Releasing Emotional Baggage:

Emotions serve as potent messengers, offering valuable insights into our inner landscape. We look into the significance of emotional healing and release in overcoming limiting beliefs and patterns, presenting techniques such as emotional processing, forgiveness practices, and energy healing modalities. These methods enable us to shed emotional baggage and heal old wounds, liberating ourselves from the grasp of past traumas and pain.

Energy Healing:

Energy Healing is often used as a complementary therapy alongside conventional medical treatments to support the body's natural healing processes and promote overall health and well-being. While scientific evidence for the effectiveness of energy healing is still emerging, many people report significant benefits, including reduced pain, improved mood, and enhanced relaxation, from receiving energy healing treatments.

Reiki: Reiki is a Japanese form of energy healing that involves the laying on of hands to channel universal life force energy to the recipient. Practitioners act as conduits for this energy, directing it to areas of the body where it is needed most to promote relaxation, reduce stress, and support the body's natural healing processes.

Chakra Balancing: In many holistic traditions, it is believed that the body has seven main energy centres called chakras, which correspond to different aspects of physical, emotional, and spiritual well-being. Chakra balancing involves using various techniques such as visualisation, breathwork, and hands-on healing to clear and balance the chakras, allowing energy to flow freely throughout the body.

Pranic Healing: Pranic healing is a form of energy healing that works with the body's energy field, known as the aura, to remove energetic blockages and promote healing. Practitioners use visualisation and specific hand movements to manipulate energy and cleanse the aura, allowing the body to restore balance and vitality.

Healing Touch: Healing touch is a gentle, non-invasive form of energy healing that involves using the hands to clear, energise, and balance the body's energy field. Practitioners may use techniques such as sweeping, grounding, and magnetic passes to facilitate healing on physical, emotional, and spiritual levels.

Quantum Healing: Quantum healing is a modern approach to energy healing that incorporates principles from quantum physics and consciousness studies. It focuses on the interconnectedness of mind, body, and spirit, using intention, visualisation, and quantum principles to facilitate healing and transformation.

Cultivating a Mindset of Empowerment:

Empowerment begins with a shift in mindset, a willingness to embrace change, take risks, and trust in our innate abilities. Here, we investigate practical strategies for cultivating a mindset of empowerment and possibility. We discuss the importance of self-love, self-compassion, and self-care in nurturing resilience and personal growth. We also explore the role of visualisation, goal setting, and inspired action in manifesting our dreams and aspirations.

Integration and Transformation:

Transformation is a gradual process that unfolds as we continue to cultivate self-awareness and take intentional steps toward personal growth, seeing the importance of integration in the journey of overcoming limiting beliefs and patterns. Integrating new beliefs and patterns into our daily lives through consistent practice, accountability, and self-reflection, ultimately fosters a sense of alignment, wholeness, and empowerment.

Cultivate Self-Awareness: Start by cultivating self-awareness through practices such as mindfulness meditation, journaling, or therapy. Take time to reflect on your thoughts, emotions, and behaviours, identifying any limiting beliefs or patterns that may be holding you back.

Identify Limiting Beliefs and Patterns: Once you've developed self-awareness, identify the specific limiting beliefs and patterns that are impacting your life. These may be beliefs such as "I'm not good enough" or patterns like self-sabotage or procrastination.

Challenge and Reframe: Challenge these limiting beliefs and patterns by questioning their validity and reframing them into more empowering beliefs. Replace "I'm not good enough" with "I am worthy and capable of success," for example.

Set Intentions for Transformation: Set clear intentions for transformation by defining the beliefs and patterns you want to integrate into your life. Visualise yourself embodying these new beliefs and behaviours and commit to taking intentional steps toward their realisation.

Practice Consistency: Integrate new beliefs and patterns into your daily life through consistent practice. This may involve repeating affirmations, engaging in positive self-talk, or implementing new behaviours that align with your desired outcomes.

Accountability and Support: Seek accountability and support from trusted friends, family members, or mentors who can help hold you accountable to your intentions for transformation. Share your goals and progress with them regularly and enlist their encouragement and feedback along the way.

Self-Reflection and Adjustment: Regularly reflect on your progress and adjust your approach as needed. Notice any resistance or setbacks that arise and use them as opportunities for growth and learning. Celebrate your successes and be compassionate with yourself during moments of challenge.

Foster Alignment and Wholeness: As you continue on your journey of integration and transformation, foster a sense of alignment and wholeness within yourself. Embrace all aspects of your being—both strengths and weaknesses—and recognise that growth is a continual process of evolution and self-discovery.

Embrace Empowerment: Ultimately, the goal of integration and transformation is to foster a sense of empowerment within yourself. Embrace your ability to create positive change in your life, and trust in your capacity to overcome limiting beliefs and patterns, leading to a life filled with alignment, wholeness, and empowerment.

By identifying and reframing limiting beliefs, releasing emotional baggage, and cultivating a mindset of empowerment, we unlock our quantum potential and pave the way for profound personal growth and transformation. In doing so, we align ourselves with the dynamic and transformative energy of the quantum realm, embracing our innate capacity for resilience, creativity, and fulfilment.

Understanding Quantum Self-Care:

Quantum self-care goes beyond traditional notions of self-care, recognising the intricate interplay between our physical, emotional, and energetic bodies, and how quantum principles inform our understanding of self-care, emphasising the importance of nurturing our entire being, mind, body, and spirit. How quantum self-care involves aligning with the natural rhythms of the universe, honouring our unique needs, and cultivating a deep sense of self-awareness and presence.

Holistic Approaches to Self-Care:

Self-care encompasses a wide range of practices that nourish and replenish our mind, body, and spirit. This is where we explore holistic approaches to self-care that integrate quantum principles and promote overall well-being. We read into the importance of nutrition as fuel for our quantum bodies, the transformative power of movement and exercise, and the restorative benefits of quality sleep. We will also discuss stress management techniques, such as mindfulness, meditation, and breathwork, that help us cultivate inner peace and resilience in the face of life's challenges.

Mind-Body-Spirit Connection: Recognise the interconnectedness of your mind, body, and spirit, and understand that holistic self-care addresses all aspects of your being. Embrace the idea that caring for one aspect of yourself positively impacts the others.

Nutrition as Fuel: Start by examining your diet and nutrition habits. Choose whole, nourishing foods that provide the essential nutrients your body needs to function optimally. Incorporate fresh fruits and vegetables, lean proteins, healthy fats, and whole grains into your meals to fuel your quantum body.

Movement and Exercise: Incorporate regular movement and exercise into your routine to promote physical health and vitality. Choose activities that you enjoy and that nourish your body, whether it's yoga, dancing, walking in nature, or strength training. Movement not only strengthens your physical body but also supports mental clarity and emotional well-being.

Quality Sleep: Prioritise quality sleep as an essential component of self-care. Create a bedtime routine that promotes relaxation and restful sleep, such as turning off electronic devices, dimming the lights, and engaging in calming activities like reading or meditation. Aim for 7-9 hours of uninterrupted sleep each night to support your body's natural healing processes.

Stress Management: Explore stress management techniques to cultivate inner peace and resilience in the face of life's challenges. Practice mindfulness meditation to bring your attention to the present moment and reduce stress levels. Incorporate breathwork exercises to calm the nervous system and promote relaxation. Engage in activities that bring you joy and help you recharge, such as spending time in nature, practicing hobbies, or connecting with loved ones.

Holistic Healing Modalities: Consider exploring holistic healing modalities that integrate quantum principles and promote overall well-being. This may include energy healing, sound therapy, acupuncture, or Reiki. These practices can help balance your energy field, release energetic blockages, and support your body's natural healing processes.

Self-Compassion and Self-Love: Cultivate self-compassion and self-love as essential components of holistic self-care. Treat yourself with kindness and understanding and prioritise activities and practices that nourish your soul and bring you joy. Practice gratitude for the blessings in your life and celebrate your achievements, no matter how small.

Consistency and Commitment: Finally, commit to incorporating holistic self-care practices into your daily life consistently. Create a self-care routine that aligns with your needs and preferences and make self-care a non-negotiable part of your daily schedule. Remember that self-care is not selfish; it is an essential investment in your overall health and well-being.

Energetic Self-Care Practices:

Our energetic body plays a crucial role in our overall well-being, influencing our physical health, emotional balance, and spiritual vitality, looking at energetic self-care practices that support our quantum essence and promote energetic balance and harmony. Discussing the importance of energy hygiene, including practices such as grounding, clearing, and balancing our energy centres (chakras). We also explore the transformative power of energy healing modalities, such as Reiki, acupuncture, and sound therapy, that help us release energetic blockages and restore flow and vitality to our being.

By incorporating energetic self-care practices into your wellness routine, you can support your quantum essence and promote energetic balance and vitality in all aspects of your being. Embrace the transformative power of energy healing modalities and cultivate a deeper connection to your energetic body, leading to a life filled with vitality, balance, and harmony.

Understanding the Energetic Body: Begin by understanding the concept of the energetic body and its influence on your overall well-being. Recognise that your energetic body interacts with your physical, emotional, and spiritual aspects, and plays a crucial role in maintaining balance and vitality.

Energy Hygiene: Explore the importance of energy hygiene in maintaining energetic balance and harmony. Learn practices such as grounding, clearing, and balancing your energy centres (chakras) to promote optimal energetic flow. Grounding techniques, such as walking barefoot in nature or visualising roots connecting you to the earth, can help you release excess energy and stay rooted in the present moment. Clearing practices, such as smudging with sage or using crystals, can help remove negative or stagnant energy from your aura. Balancing practices, such as meditation or working with specific yoga poses, can help align and harmonise your chakras, ensuring smooth energy flow throughout your body.

Exploring Energy Healing Modalities: Dive into the transformative power of energy healing modalities that support your energetic essence and promote well-being. Explore practices such as Reiki, acupuncture, and sound therapy, which help release energetic blockages and restore flow and vitality to your being. Reiki involves the channelling of universal life force energy to promote healing and balance in the body. Acupuncture works by stimulating specific points on the body to regulate the flow of energy and promote holistic healing. Sound therapy uses vibrations and frequencies to harmonise the body's energy field and induce deep relaxation and healing.

Self-Practice and Exploration: Take time to engage in energetic self-care practices regularly and explore what resonates most with you. Experiment with different grounding techniques, clearing rituals, and energy healing modalities to find what works best for your unique needs and preferences. Listen to your intuition and trust your inner guidance as you navigate your energetic journey.

Seeking Guidance and Support: Consider seeking guidance and support from experienced practitioners or teachers who can offer insights and techniques to deepen your energetic self-care practice. Attend workshops, classes, or retreats focused on energy healing and holistic wellness to expand your knowledge and skills in this area. Connect with like-minded individuals who share your interest in energetic self-care and exchange experiences and resources.

Integration and Reflection: Integrate energetic self-care practices into your daily life and reflect on their impact on your overall well-being. Notice any shifts or changes in your physical health, emotional balance, and spiritual vitality as you engage in these practices regularly. Be patient and compassionate with yourself as you navigate your energetic journey, trusting that each step brings you closer to greater alignment and harmony.

Cultivating Mindfulness in Everyday Life:

Mindfulness is a cornerstone of quantum self-care, inviting us to cultivate present moment awareness and deepen our connection to the here and now. Using practical strategies for integrating mindfulness into our daily lives, allows us to savour the richness of each moment and experience life more fully. The benefits of mindfulness practices such as mindful eating, mindful movement, and mindful communication, these practices can enhance our overall well-being and resilience.

Nurturing the Quantum Self:

As we nurture our quantum essence through self-care practices, we align ourselves with the inherent wisdom and vitality of the quantum realm. Going forward we reflect on the importance of self-compassion, self-love, and self-acceptance in the journey of quantum self-care. Cultivating a deep sense of self-compassion allows us to honour our inherent worth and embrace our imperfections with kindness and understanding. The power of self-love as a transformative force empowers us to live authentically and wholeheartedly, embracing our true essence and to shine brightly in the world.

By nurturing your quantum essence through self-care practices and embracing self-compassion and self-love, you align with the inherent wisdom and vitality of the quantum realm, and empower yourself to live a life of authenticity, joy, and purpose. Embrace the journey of quantum self-care with an open heart and a spirit of curiosity and exploration, knowing that you are worthy of love and belonging, exactly as you are.

Nurturing Your Quantum Essence: Begin by recognising the importance of nurturing your quantum essence through self-care practices. Understand that you are inherently connected to the wisdom and vitality of the quantum realm, and that by caring for yourself, you align with this inherent wisdom and vitality. Engage in practices such as mindfulness, meditation, movement, and energy healing to nourish your mind, body, and spirit on a quantum level.

Reflecting on Self-Compassion, Self-Love, and Self-Acceptance: Take time to reflect on the importance of self-compassion, self-love, and self-acceptance in your journey of quantum self-care. Understand that these qualities are essential for cultivating a deep sense of inner peace, resilience, and well-being. Recognise that self-compassion allows you to honour your inherent worth and embrace your imperfections with kindness and understanding.

Cultivating Self-Compassion: Explore practical ways to cultivate self-compassion in your daily life. Practice self-kindness by speaking to yourself with the same warmth and understanding that you would offer to a dear friend. Embrace self-compassionate language and thoughts and challenge your inner critic with compassion and empathy. Remember that self-compassion is not about being perfect, but about embracing your humanity and treating yourself with kindness and care.

Harnessing the Power of Self-Love: Embrace self-love as a transformative force that empowers you to live authentically and wholeheartedly. Recognise that self-love is not selfish or indulgent, but essential for your well-being and growth. Practice acts of self-love daily, such as setting boundaries, prioritising your needs, and engaging in activities that bring you joy and fulfilment. Embrace your true essence and shine brightly in the world, knowing that you are worthy of love and belonging just as you are.

Integration and Application: Integrate self-compassion and self-love into your quantum self-care routine and apply these qualities to all aspects of your life. Notice how cultivating self-compassion and self-love enhances your overall well-being and relationships and celebrate the progress you make along the way. Be patient and gentle with yourself as you navigate your journey of quantum self-care, knowing that each step brings you closer to living a life of alignment, authenticity, and fulfilment.

Integration and Transformation:

By integrating holistic self-care practices into your daily lives, you can cultivate resilience, vitality, and inner peace, allowing you to thrive in all areas of life. In doing so, you align yourselves with the dynamic and harmonious energy of the quantum realm, honouring your true essence and living with intention, purpose, and joy.

Within this segment, we explore the inspiring narratives of individuals who have exemplified the principles of quantum resilience, showcasing remarkable strength, courage, and adaptability amid adversity. Through their journeys, we unearth valuable insights and lessons that highlight the transformative potential of resilience and provide guidance for gracefully navigating life's challenges.

Real-Life Examples of Quantum Resilience:

These real-life examples illustrate the transformative power of quantum resilience in action, demonstrating how individuals can overcome personal hardships and professional setbacks with courage, perseverance, and unwavering belief in themselves. Through their inspiring stories, they remind us that resilience is not just about bouncing back from adversity but also about using challenges as opportunities for growth and positive change.

Nick Vujicic: Overcoming Physical Challenges with Resilience

Nick Vujicic was born without arms or legs, facing profound physical challenges from birth. Despite his disabilities, Nick refused to let his circumstances define him. Through unwavering resilience and determination, he learned to adapt and thrive in a world that often seemed stacked against him. Today, Nick is a motivational speaker, author, and advocate for people with disabilities, inspiring millions with his message of hope, resilience, and the power of a positive mindset.

J.K. Rowling: From Rejection to Success

Before J.K. Rowling became one of the most successful authors of all time with her "Harry Potter" series, she faced numerous rejections and setbacks in her writing career. Rowling endured personal hardships, including divorce and financial struggles, while raising her daughter as a single mother. Despite these challenges, she persisted in pursuing her passion for writing, channelling her resilience and creativity into the creation of the magical world of Hogwarts. Today, Rowling's story serves as a testament to the transformative power of resilience, perseverance, and belief in oneself.

Malala Yousafzai: Defying Adversity for Education

Malala Yousafzai, a Pakistani activist for female education, survived an assassination attempt by the Taliban at the age of 15. Despite facing grave danger for advocating for girls' rights to education, Malala refused to be silenced. Her resilience in the face of adversity only strengthened her resolve to fight for the rights of girls and women worldwide. Malala went on to become the youngest-ever Nobel Prize laureate, using her platform to champion education as a fundamental human right and inspire millions to stand up for equality and justice.

Nelson Mandela: Leading with Resilience in the Face of Oppression

Nelson Mandela, South Africa's first black president, spent 27 years in prison for his anti-apartheid activism. Despite enduring unimaginable hardships and facing systemic oppression, Mandela remained steadfast in his commitment to justice, equality, and reconciliation. Upon his release from prison, Mandela emerged as a symbol of hope and resilience, leading South Africa through a peaceful transition to democracy. His resilience in the face of adversity and his unwavering belief in the power of forgiveness and reconciliation continue to inspire generations around the world.

Bethany Hamilton: Surfer's Resilience After Shark Attack

Bethany Hamilton, a professional surfer, lost her left arm in a shark attack at the age of 13. Despite the traumatic incident, Bethany refused to let it derail her dreams of surfing competitively. With determination and resilience, she returned to the water just weeks after the attack and continued to pursue her passion for surfing. Bethany's resilience and courage in overcoming adversity propelled her to become one of the most successful female surfers in the world, inspiring others to persevere in the face of challenges.

Navigating Personal Challenges:

Here are some stories of individuals who have faced profound personal challenges, such as illness, loss, or trauma, and emerged stronger and more resilient on the other side. We see how these individuals navigated their darkest moments with courage and resilience, drawing upon their inner resources and support networks to find healing, growth, and renewal. Their stories serve as powerful reminders of the human capacity for resilience and the transformative potential of adversity.

Gabrielle Union: Overcoming Trauma and Advocating for Change

Actress Gabrielle Union has been vocal about her experience surviving sexual assault at gunpoint and the subsequent trauma she endured. Instead of allowing this experience to define her, Union has become an outspoken advocate for survivors of sexual violence. Through therapy, self-care practices, and activism, she has used her platform to raise awareness, promote healing, and empower others to speak out against sexual abuse.

Michael J. Fox: Living with Parkinson's Disease

Actor Michael J. Fox was diagnosed with Parkinson's disease at the age of 29, forcing him to confront significant physical and emotional challenges. Despite the progressive nature of the disease, Fox has remained resilient, using his diagnosis as a catalyst for positive change. He established the Michael J. Fox Foundation for Parkinson's Research, which has funded groundbreaking research and raised awareness about the condition. Fox's resilience in the face of adversity has inspired millions and transformed the landscape of Parkinson's research and treatment.

Sheryl Sandberg: Finding Resilience After Loss

Facebook COO Sheryl Sandberg faced a devastating personal loss when her husband, Dave Goldberg, unexpectedly passed away. In the aftermath of her husband's death, Sandberg navigated grief with courage and resilience, drawing upon her inner strength and support network to find healing and renewal. She authored the book "Option B: Facing Adversity, Building Resilience, and Finding Joy," which shares her journey of resilience and offers practical advice for others navigating loss and hardship.

Demi Lovato: Overcoming Addiction and Mental Health Challenges

Singer-songwriter Demi Lovato has been open about her struggles with addiction, eating disorders, and mental health issues. Despite facing numerous setbacks and relapses, Lovato has remained committed to her recovery journey and advocating for mental health awareness. She has used her platform to destigmatise discussions around mental illness and encourage others to seek help. Lovato's resilience in overcoming personal challenges serves as a source of inspiration for millions struggling with similar issues.

Jay Shetty: Transforming Trauma into Empowerment

Former monk turned motivational speaker Jay Shetty experienced childhood trauma and struggled with his mental health as a young adult. Instead of succumbing to despair, Shetty embarked on a journey of self-discovery and personal growth, delving into mindfulness practices and spiritual teachings. Today, he shares his insights and wisdom through his books, podcasts, and social media platforms, inspiring others to transform their pain into purpose and find inner peace and fulfilment.

Overcoming Professional Setbacks:

Next, we read into stories of individuals who have encountered professional setbacks or career challenges and used them as opportunities for growth and self-discovery. Whether facing job loss, business failure, or career transitions, these individuals have demonstrated resilience in the face of uncertainty, embracing change and reinventing themselves in pursuit of their dreams. Through their determination, resourcefulness, and resilience, they have turned setbacks into stepping stones and emerged stronger and more successful than ever before.

Walt Disney: Turning Failure into Success

Before creating the iconic Disney empire, Walt Disney faced numerous setbacks and failures. He was fired from his job as a newspaper editor for lacking creativity and went bankrupt several times while attempting to start his own businesses. Despite these challenges, Disney remained resilient and determined to pursue his passion for animation. He eventually found success with the creation of Mickey Mouse and went on to build one of the most influential entertainment companies in the world.

Steve Jobs: Bouncing Back from Failure

Apple co-founder Steve Jobs experienced numerous setbacks and failures throughout his career, including being ousted from his own company in the 1980s. Despite this setback, Jobs remained resilient and used his time away from Apple to launch other successful ventures, including Pixar Animation Studios. He eventually returned to Apple and led the company to unprecedented success with the creation of groundbreaking products such as the iPhone and iPad. Jobs' resilience and willingness to embrace change played a significant role in his ability to bounce back from failure and achieve success.

Colonel Sanders: Finding Success Later in Life

Colonel Harland Sanders, the founder of Kentucky Fried Chicken (KFC), faced a series of professional setbacks throughout his life. He experienced multiple business failures, including the bankruptcy of his first restaurant, and struggled to make ends meet in his later years. However, Sanders remained resilient and determined to succeed. At the age of 65, he franchised his secret recipe for fried chicken, which eventually became the foundation of the KFC empire. Sanders' story serves as a testament to the power of resilience and perseverance in the face of adversity.

Vera Wang: From Figure Skater to Fashion Icon

Vera Wang initially pursued a career as a competitive figure skater but failed to make the Olympic team. Despite this setback, she transitioned into the fashion industry, working as a fashion editor for Vogue magazine. However, when she was passed over for the editor-in-chief position, Wang decided to pursue her dream of becoming a fashion designer. She

launched her own bridalwear company at the age of 40, and today, Vera Wang is one of the most renowned fashion designers in the world, known for her elegant and timeless designs.

Elon Musk: Reimagining the Future

Elon Musk, the CEO of SpaceX and Tesla, has faced numerous setbacks and failures throughout his career. From the early days of SpaceX, when his rockets failed to reach orbit, to the production challenges at Tesla, Musk has encountered numerous obstacles on his path to success. However, he has consistently demonstrated resilience and determination, pushing through adversity to achieve his ambitious goals of revolutionising space travel and sustainable energy. Musk's unwavering belief in his vision and willingness to take risks have made him one of the most influential entrepreneurs of the 21st century.

Embracing Resilience as a Way of Life:

As we reflect on these inspiring stories of quantum resilience in action, we recognise that resilience is not merely a response to adversity but a way of life, a mindset and a skill set that can be cultivated and strengthened over time. By embracing resilience as a guiding principle in our lives, we empower ourselves to navigate life's ups and downs with courage, grace, and fortitude, knowing that we have the inner resources and resilience to overcome any obstacle that comes our way.

Integration and Application:

We ask you to reflect on your own experiences of resilience and consider how you can apply the lessons learned from these inspiring stories to your own life. By cultivating a mindset of resilience, embracing change, and tapping into your inner strength and resourcefulness, you can navigate life's challenges with confidence and resilience, knowing that you have the power to overcome adversity and create positive change in your life.

Reflecting on the Essence of Quantum Resilience

Quantum resilience is not merely about bouncing back from adversity; it's about embracing the inherent uncertainty of existence with unwavering courage and fortitude. It's acknowledging that, much like the quantum realm itself, our lives are governed by probabilities and uncertainties. Every moment is imbued with potentiality, offering us countless paths to traverse and choices to make.

Reflect on the image of a quantum particle, oscillating between states of existence until observed or measured. Similarly, we, too, oscillate between states of being, sometimes thriving, sometimes faltering, but always in a state of flux. Embracing quantum resilience entails recognising this inherent dynamism and learning to navigate the waves of change with grace and resilience.

Cultivating Resilience with Courage and Compassion

At the heart of quantum resilience lies the courage to confront adversity head-on, to embrace challenges as opportunities for growth rather than obstacles to be feared. It's about stepping into the unknown with a sense of adventure, knowing that within every challenge lies the potential for transformation.

But courage alone is not enough. We must also cultivate compassion, for ourselves and for others, as we navigate the tumultuous seas of life. Compassion softens the edges of adversity, infusing our journey with empathy and understanding. It reminds us that we are all flawed beings, bound together by our shared humanity and our collective struggle for meaning and purpose.

Viewing Challenges as Opportunities for Growth

In the quantum realm, uncertainty is not a hindrance; it's a fundamental aspect of reality. Similarly, in our lives, challenges are not roadblocks; they are stepping stones on the path to self-discovery and enlightenment. Each setback, each moment of discomfort, presents us with an opportunity to learn, to adapt, and to evolve.

Approach life with the mindset of an explorer, venturing into uncharted territories with a sense of wonder and awe and embrace the unknown with open arms, knowing that within its vast expanse lies the potential for infinite growth and transformation.

In conclusion, embracing quantum resilience is not merely a choice; it's a way of life, a philosophy that empowers us to navigate the complexities of existence with grace and resilience. So, let us enjoy this journey with courage, compassion, and a sense of adventure, knowing that each challenge is but a stepping stone on the path to self-realisation and fulfilment.

Chapter 6: Quantum Connection

In the intricate web of existence, there exists a profound truth that transcends the boundaries of space and time: quantum connection. It is the recognition that all beings, from the smallest subatomic particles to the vast expanse of the cosmos, are interconnected at a fundamental level. In this chapter, we embark on a journey to explore the essence of quantum connection and its implications for our understanding of unity, compassion, and manifestation.

Unravelling the Essence of Quantum Connection

At its core, quantum connection is a fundamental principle of quantum physics, rooted in the concept of entanglement. Entanglement suggests that particles once in proximity can become correlated in such a way that the state of one particle instantaneously influences the state of another, regardless of the distance separating them. This phenomenon underscores the inseparable bond that exists between all particles in the universe, highlighting the interconnected nature of reality itself.

But quantum connection extends far beyond the realm of subatomic particles. It permeates every facet of existence, from the microscopic to the macroscopic, weaving a tapestry of interdependence that binds all beings together in a delicate dance of cosmic harmony. It is a reminder that, despite our perceived separateness, we are all threads in the fabric of the universe, each intricately connected to the whole.

Illuminating the Path to Unity and Compassion

The recognition of quantum connection serves as a catalyst for cultivating unity and compassion in our lives. When we acknowledge that we are all interconnected, we begin to see ourselves reflected in the eyes of others, recognising the inherent worth and dignity of every being. This realisation fosters a sense of empathy and understanding, bridging the perceived divide between self and other.

Moreover, quantum connection underscores the interdependence of all living beings, highlighting the ripple effect of our actions and choices on the world around us. Just as a pebble dropped into a pond sends out concentric waves, so too do our thoughts, words, and deeds reverberate throughout the interconnected web of existence. This awareness compels us to act with kindness and compassion, knowing that our individual actions have the power to shape the collective destiny of humanity.

Harnessing Quantum Connection for Manifestation

In the realm of manifestation, quantum connection plays a pivotal role in shaping our reality. By recognising the interconnected nature of all things, we begin to understand that our thoughts and intentions have the power to influence the world around us. Just as the observer influences the observed in quantum mechanics, so too do our perceptions and beliefs shape the unfolding of events in our lives.

Embracing quantum connection as a foundational principle of manifestation empowers us to co-create our reality in alignment with our deepest desires and aspirations. By cultivating a sense of unity and interconnectedness with the universe, we open ourselves to the infinite possibilities that lie beyond the confines of our limited perceptions. We become conscious co-creators of our destiny, harnessing the power of quantum connection to manifest our dreams into reality.

As a result, quantum connection is not merely a theoretical concept; it is a profound truth that lies at the heart of existence itself. By welcoming the interconnected nature of reality, we awaken to the inherent unity and compassion that bind us together as one. And through the conscious application of this principle, we unlock the power of manifestation, harnessing the infinite potential of the universe to create a life of purpose, abundance, and fulfilment.

In the seemingly chaotic dance of particles and waves that make up the quantum realm, there exists a hidden order, a profound interconnectedness that transcends the boundaries of space and time.

Unveiling the Dance of Quantum Interconnectedness

At the heart of quantum physics lies the principle of entanglement, an enigmatic phenomenon that links particles together in a state of inseparable correlation. When two particles become entangled, the state of one particle instantaneously influences the state of the other, regardless of the distance separating them. This baffling interconnectedness defies our classical notions of cause and effect, revealing a deeper layer of reality governed by quantum entanglement.

But entanglement is not confined to the realm of subatomic particles; it extends to larger systems as well. Complex quantum systems, such as atoms, molecules, and even living organisms, can become entangled with one another, forming intricate networks of interconnectedness that span the breadth of existence. This interconnectedness gives rise to emergent phenomena and collective behaviours that defy reductionist explanations, highlighting the holistic nature of reality.

Bridging the Gulf Between Quantum and Macroscopic Worlds

While the effects of quantum interconnectedness may seem confined to the microscopic realm, they reverberate throughout the fabric of the universe, shaping the macroscopic world in profound ways. Quantum coherence, the phenomenon of particles maintaining correlation over large distances, can give rise to macroscopic effects such as superconductivity and superfluidity, which have far-reaching implications for technology and fundamental science.

Moreover, the interconnectedness observed in the quantum realm mirrors the interconnectedness of human relationships and collective consciousness. Just as particles become entangled through interactions, so too do individuals become entwined through shared experiences, emotions, and intentions. This interconnectedness forms the basis of empathy, compassion, and cooperation, fostering a sense of unity and belonging within the human family.

Embracing Interconnectedness for Personal and Planetary Transformation

As we deepen our understanding of interconnectedness in the quantum realm, we come to recognise its profound implications for personal and planetary transformation. By embracing the interconnected nature of reality, we cultivate a sense of empathy and compassion for all beings, recognising that we are all interconnected threads in the fabric of existence.

Moreover, by harnessing the power of quantum interconnectedness, we can effect positive change in the world around us. Through conscious intention and collective action, we can amplify the ripple effects of our thoughts and deeds, catalysing a shift toward a more harmonious and sustainable world. By aligning ourselves with the deeper rhythms of the universe, we become co-creators of our destiny, weaving a tapestry of interconnectedness that transcends the boundaries of time and space.

Overall, the exploration of interconnectedness in the quantum realm reveals a hidden unity that permeates the fabric of existence. By using this interconnectedness, we awaken to the intrinsic bond that unites all beings, fostering a sense of unity, compassion, and cooperation. And through the conscious application of this principle, we can harness the power of interconnectedness to catalyse personal and planetary transformation, ushering in a new era of harmony, abundance, and well-being for all.

In the boundless expanse of the cosmos, amidst the swirling dance of particles and waves, there exists a profound truth that transcends the limitations of individuality, a truth known as unity consciousness. It is the recognition that at the deepest level of reality, we are all interconnected, interdependent expressions of the same cosmic tapestry.

Delving into the Essence of Unity Consciousness

Unity consciousness is not merely a philosophical concept; it is a fundamental truth that lies at the heart of existence itself. It is the understanding that beneath the veneer of separation and division, there exists a hidden unity, an interconnectedness that binds all beings together in a web of cosmic kinship. In the words of the ancient wisdom traditions, "We are all one."

At its core, unity consciousness is a shift in perception, a recognition of the underlying unity that permeates the fabric of reality. It is a journey from the illusion of separateness to the realisation of oneness, a journey that transcends the boundaries of space and time, awakening us to the inherent interconnectedness of all things.

Fostering Belonging, Compassion, and Empathy

When we accept unity consciousness, we awaken to a profound sense of belonging, a recognition that we are not separate entities adrift in an indifferent universe, but integral parts of a larger whole. This sense of belonging fosters a deep sense of security and connection, alleviating the existential loneliness that plagues so many in our modern world.

Moreover, acknowledging our deep connection with others fosters compassion and empathy for all beings. When we recognise our common humanity in the eyes of others, we cannot ignore their suffering. Instead, we feel compelled to extend a helping hand, providing comfort and assistance to those in need. Compassion transcends being merely a virtue; it becomes integral to our way of life, reflecting our shared humanity and interconnected existence.

Nurturing Personal and Collective Evolution

Unity consciousness is not merely a lofty ideal; it is a catalyst for personal and collective evolution. By recognising our interconnectedness, we transcend the limitations of ego and embrace the fullness of our being. We realise that the well-being of one is intricately linked to the well-being of all, and that true fulfilment comes not from the pursuit of individual gain, but from the cultivation of a more harmonious and compassionate world.

Moreover, as we collectively awaken to unity consciousness, we usher in a new era of planetary evolution, a shift from competition to cooperation, from exploitation to stewardship. We see that we are custodians of this precious planet, entrusted with the task of nurturing and preserving the delicate balance of life. And through our collective actions and intentions, we can co-create a world that honours our interconnectedness and celebrates the diversity of all living beings.

By recognising our connections, we foster a sense of belonging, compassion, and empathy for all beings. And through the conscious application of this principle, we can usher in a new era of harmony, abundance, and well-being for all.

In the hustle and bustle of modern life, amidst the cacophony of competing demands and distractions, it can be easy to lose sight of what truly matters, our shared humanity, our capacity for compassion and empathy. In this segment, we embark on an exploration of practical strategies for fostering compassion and empathy in our daily lives. We draw inspiration from mindfulness practices, loving-kindness meditation, and acts of service that cultivate a profound sense of connection and altruism.

The Power of Compassion and Empathy

Compassion and empathy are not mere abstract concepts; they are transformative forces that have the power to heal, to uplift, and to unite. Compassion is the ability to recognise and alleviate the suffering of others, while empathy is the capacity to understand and share in the feelings of others. Together, they form the foundation of our moral and ethical compass, guiding us on the path of kindness, generosity, and love.

Embracing Mindfulness as a Path to Compassion

At the heart of cultivating compassion and empathy lies the practice of mindfulness, a state of open-hearted awareness that allows us to fully engage with the present moment, free from judgment or distraction. Through mindfulness, we learn to cultivate a deep sense of presence and connection with ourselves and others, fostering empathy and compassion for all beings.

Practicing Loving-Kindness Meditation

Loving-kindness meditation, or metta meditation, is a powerful tool for cultivating compassion and empathy. In this practice, we cultivate feelings of love, kindness, and goodwill toward ourselves and others, extending our heartfelt wishes for happiness and well-being to all beings, without exception.

Engaging in Acts of Service and Altruism

Finally, acts of service and altruism offer tangible ways to express compassion and empathy in action. Whether volunteering at a local charity, lending a helping hand to a friend in need, or simply offering a kind word or gesture to a stranger, acts of service allow us to embody the principles of compassion and empathy in our daily lives, fostering a sense of connection and solidarity with all beings.

To sum up, cultivating compassion and empathy is not just a personal practice; it is a way of being in the world, a way of embodying our deepest values and aspirations. By embracing mindfulness, loving-kindness meditation, and acts of service, we can cultivate a more compassionate and empathetic world, where kindness, generosity, and love reign supreme.

And through our collective efforts, we can usher in a new era of harmony, compassion, and well-being for all.

In the vast tapestry of human interaction, communication serves as the lifeblood that connects us, shapes our relationships, and influences the trajectory of our lives. Yet, beneath the surface of our verbal exchanges and social interactions lies a deeper realm, a realm informed by the principles of quantum physics, where nonverbal cues, energetic exchanges, and subtle connections play a pivotal role in shaping our reality.

Understanding Quantum Principles in Communication

In the realm of quantum physics, communication takes on a new dimension, one that transcends the limitations of classical mechanics and embraces the interconnected nature of reality. Just as particles become entangled through interactions, so too do individuals become entwined through shared experiences, emotions, and intentions. This entanglement forms the basis of quantum communication, where information is exchanged through subtle energetic interactions that transcend the confines of space and time.

The Role of Nonverbal Cues and Energetic Exchanges

While verbal communication forms the basis of our social interactions, it is often the nonverbal cues and energetic exchanges that convey the true depth of our thoughts and feelings. From the subtle nuances of body language to the intangible vibrations of energy that permeate our interactions, these nonverbal cues serve as a rich tapestry of information, revealing hidden truths and forging deep connections between individuals.

Harnessing Subtle Connections for Manifestation

In the realm of manifestation, quantum communication plays a pivotal role in shaping our reality. Just as particles respond to the observer's gaze in quantum mechanics, so too do our thoughts, emotions, and intentions influence the unfolding of events in our lives. By harnessing the power of subtle connections and energetic exchanges, we can amplify the potency of our manifestations, aligning ourselves with the flow of the universe and co-creating our reality in harmony with our deepest desires and aspirations.

Embracing Quantum Communication in Relationships

In our relationships, quantum communication offers a pathway to deeper connection and intimacy. By attuning ourselves to the subtle cues and energetic vibrations that underlie our interactions, we can cultivate a greater sense of empathy, understanding, and compassion for those around us. This heightened awareness allows us to communicate more authentically, fostering a sense of trust and intimacy that transcends the limitations of words alone.

To summarise, quantum communication offers a profound paradigm shift in our understanding of relationships and manifestation. By adopting the principles of quantum physics, we can unlock the hidden potential of nonverbal cues, energetic exchanges, and subtle connections, transforming our interactions and shaping our reality in alignment with our highest aspirations. And through the conscious application of these principles, we can cultivate deeper connections, manifest our desires, and co-create a world of harmony, abundance, and fulfilment.

In the intricate tapestry of existence, there exists a hidden realm, a realm shaped by the collective thoughts, beliefs, and intentions of humanity, a realm known as collective consciousness. We will discover the profound role of collective consciousness in manifestation and social change, and how aligning with the collective intention can amplify individual manifestation efforts and contribute to larger-scale transformation.

Understanding Collective Consciousness

Collective consciousness is the shared pool of thoughts, beliefs, and values that permeates the collective psyche of humanity. It is the total of our shared experiences, aspirations, and cultural heritage, a living, breathing entity that shapes our perceptions, behaviours, and reality itself. Just as individual thoughts and intentions influence the unfolding of events in our lives, so too do collective thoughts and intentions shape the course of history.

The Role of Collective Consciousness in Manifestation

In the realm of manifestation, collective consciousness plays a crucial role in shaping our reality. Just as a solitary action creates ripples that extend outward, our individual manifestations also send out waves, impacting the collective consciousness of humanity. When a sufficient number of individuals align their thoughts and intentions with a shared vision or purpose, a tipping point is reached, and the collective consciousness undergoes a transformation, bringing that vision to fruition.

Amplifying Individual Manifestation Efforts

By aligning with the collective intention, we can amplify our individual manifestation efforts and catalyse larger-scale transformation. When we harness the power of collective consciousness, our manifestations become more potent, more aligned with the flow of the universe, and more likely to manifest in our lives. Moreover, by joining forces with like-minded individuals and communities, we can co-create a ripple effect of positive change that transcends the limitations of individual effort.

Contributing to Larger-Scale Transformation

Ultimately, aligning with the collective intention is not just about manifesting our individual desires; it's about contributing to larger-scale transformation, for ourselves, for humanity, and for the planet. When we come together with a shared vision of peace, harmony, and abundance, we become agents of change, ushering in a new era of collective evolution and planetary well-being. Through our collective efforts, we can co-create a world that honours our interconnectedness, celebrates our diversity, and fosters a sense of unity and belonging for all beings.

Collective consciousness is a potent force that shapes our reality and influences the course of history. By aligning with the collective intention, we can amplify our individual manifestation efforts and contribute to larger-scale transformation. And through our collective actions and intentions, we can co-create a world of harmony, abundance, and fulfilment, where the highest aspirations of humanity are realised, and all beings thrive in unity and love.

In the intricate dance of existence, amidst the ebb and flow of life's tides, there exists a profound truth, a truth that transcends the boundaries of space and time, a truth known as quantum connection. We discover the profound implications of quantum connection for well-being and happiness, in ways which cultivates a sense of connection and belonging, contributing to our overall mental, emotional, and physical well-being.

The Power of Connection and Belonging

At its core, human beings are social creatures, we thrive on connection, belonging, and community. When we cultivate a sense of connection with others, we experience a deep sense of belonging, a feeling of being seen, heard, and valued for who we are. This sense of connection nourishes our souls, fuels our spirits, and contributes to our overall sense of well-being and happiness.

The Impact of Loneliness and Isolation

Conversely, when we experience loneliness and isolation, our well-being suffers. Research has shown that chronic loneliness is associated with a myriad of negative health outcomes, including increased risk of depression, anxiety, cardiovascular disease, and even premature mortality. Moreover, loneliness can impact our immune function, sleep quality, and cognitive function, further exacerbating the toll on our physical and mental health.

Strategies for Fostering Meaningful Connections

Considering the profound impact of connection on well-being, it is essential to cultivate meaningful connections in our lives. This can be achieved through a variety of strategies, including:

1. Nurturing existing relationships: Invest time and energy in nurturing your existing relationships with friends, family, and loved ones. Make an effort to stay connected, reach out regularly, and show appreciation for the people in your life.

2. Seeking out community: Join clubs, organisations, or groups that align with your interests and values. Surround yourself with like-minded individuals who share your passions and aspirations and cultivate a sense of belonging within these communities.

3. Practicing empathy and compassion: Cultivate empathy and compassion for others and seek to understand their perspectives and experiences. By fostering a sense of connection and understanding with those around you, you can deepen your relationships and create a supportive network of social support.

4. Engaging in acts of kindness: Practice random acts of kindness and generosity toward others. Whether it's offering a helping hand to a stranger, volunteering your time for a worthy cause, or simply offering a listening ear to a friend in need, acts of kindness can strengthen social bonds and foster a sense of connection and belonging.

Cultivating a sense of connection and belonging is essential for our overall well-being and happiness. By nurturing meaningful connections in our lives and fostering a sense of belonging within our communities, we can cultivate a deep sense of fulfilment, joy, and resilience that enriches every aspect of our existence. And through our collective efforts to foster connection and compassion, we can create a world where all beings thrive in harmony and love.

In the intricate web of existence, where particles dance and waves ripple across the fabric of reality, there exists a profound relationship, a relationship between the quantum realm and the ecological systems that sustain life on our planet.

Quantum Principles and Ecology

At its core, ecology is the study of the interrelationships between organisms and their environment, a field that encompasses the intricate web of life that sustains ecosystems around the globe. Quantum principles, with their emphasis on interconnectedness, uncertainty, and emergence, offer profound insights into the dynamics of ecological systems and the delicate balance that governs life on Earth.

Recognising Interconnectedness with Nature

Central to quantum ecology is the recognition of our interconnectedness with nature, that we are not separate from the natural world, but integral parts of a larger whole. Just as particles become entangled through interactions, so too are we entwined with the web of life that surrounds us. This recognition fosters a sense of reverence and respect for the natural world, inspiring us to cultivate a deeper connection with the Earth and all its inhabitants.

Fostering Responsibility and Sustainable Living

By acknowledging our interconnectedness with nature, we also embrace a sense of responsibility for its stewardship. We recognise that our actions have far-reaching consequences that ripple outwards, affecting the balance and well-being of ecosystems around the globe. This awareness inspires us to adopt sustainable living practices that minimise our ecological footprint and honour the delicate balance of life on Earth.

Embracing Quantum-Inspired Environmentalism

Quantum-inspired environmentalism is not just about reducing our impact on the planet; it's about cultivating a deeper relationship with nature and co-creating a more harmonious and sustainable world. It's about recognising that we are not separate from the Earth, but interconnected threads in the intricate tapestry of life. By embracing quantum principles and aligning our actions with the rhythms of the natural world, we can foster a deeper sense of connection, responsibility, and reverence for the Earth and all its inhabitants.

Quantum ecology offers profound insights into the interconnectedness of all life and the delicate balance that governs ecosystems around the globe. By recognising our interconnectedness with nature and embracing sustainable living practices, we can become stewards of the Earth, co-creating a more harmonious and sustainable world for future generations. And through our collective efforts to honour the web of life that sustains us, we can foster a deeper sense of connection, responsibility, and reverence for the Earth and all its inhabitants.

In the vast landscape of human experience, the principle of quantum connection serves as a guiding thread, a thread that weaves together the fabric of reality, linking individuals, communities, and the cosmos itself. As we probe into real-life examples and case studies that illustrate the transformative power of quantum connection, exploring how individuals and communities have tapped into this power to manifest desires, foster resilience, and create positive change.

These real-life success stories illustrate the transformative power of quantum connection, showing how individuals and communities have tapped into this principle to manifest desires, foster resilience, and create positive change in the world. By recognising our inherent interconnectedness and harnessing the power of collective intention, we can shape a more harmonious and compassionate world for ourselves and future generations.

The Butterfly Effect: Ripple of Kindness

The principle of quantum connection serves as a guiding thread, a thread that weaves together the fabric of reality, linking individuals, communities, and the cosmos itself. One example of this is the concept of the butterfly effect, where small acts of kindness or positive actions can create ripple effects that spread far and wide. For instance, a simple act of generosity, such as buying a meal for someone in need, can inspire others to pay it forward, creating a chain reaction of kindness that touches countless lives.

Global Meditation Events: Uniting Consciousness

As we probe into real-life examples and case studies that illustrate the transformative power of quantum connection, we see how global meditation events have demonstrated the collective power of consciousness to create positive change on a global scale. Events like the Global Peace Meditation, where millions of people come together to meditate for peace and harmony, have been shown to reduce crime rates, decrease violence, and promote social cohesion in communities around the world. These events highlight the interconnectedness of humanity and the profound impact that collective intention can have on shaping reality.

Community Healing Circles: Shared Resilience

Individuals and communities have tapped into the power of quantum connection, examples of community healing circles demonstrate the transformative power of collective healing and resilience. These circles provide a safe space for individuals to come together and share their experiences, traumas, and challenges, while also offering support, empathy, and understanding.

Through the power of shared vulnerability and connection, participants in these circles find healing, strength, and resilience to overcome adversity and create positive change in their lives and communities.

Environmental Conservation Movements: Global Unity

The principle of quantum connection is evident in global environmental conservation movements that unite people from diverse backgrounds and cultures in the shared goal of protecting our planet. Examples such as the Paris Agreement, where countries around the world come together to address climate change and promote sustainability, demonstrate how interconnectedness and collective action can drive meaningful change on a global scale. By recognising our inherent connection to the Earth and each other, these movements inspire individuals and communities to take action and create a more sustainable and harmonious world.

Scientific Research: Quantum Entanglement

Individuals and communities have tapped into the power of quantum connection as scientific research illuminates the phenomenon of quantum entanglement. Quantum entanglement is a principle of quantum mechanics where particles become interconnected regardless of the distance between them, suggesting a fundamental interconnectedness at the most fundamental level of reality. Research in this field has profound implications for our understanding of consciousness, interconnectedness, and the nature of reality, highlighting the interconnectedness of all things in the universe.

The Power of Intentional Communities

Intentional communities, such as ecovillages, co-housing communities, and intentional living communities, offer a living example of quantum connection in action. By coming together with a shared vision and intention, these communities create a fertile ground for manifestation, fostering a sense of unity, collaboration, and mutual support that empowers individuals to realise their dreams and aspirations.

Collective Healing and Transformation

In times of crisis and adversity, quantum connection can serve as a powerful catalyst for collective healing and transformation. Case studies from around the world illustrate how communities have come together in times of need, whether in response to natural disasters, social injustices, or environmental crises, to harness the power of connection and co-create a more resilient and sustainable future.

Quantum Connection in Everyday Life

Even in the midst of our daily lives, quantum connection is at work, shaping our interactions, relationships, and experiences in profound ways. Individuals have tapped into the power of connection to manifest desires, foster resilience, and create positive change in their personal and professional lives. From the power of networking and collaboration to the transformative potential of mentorship and community support, quantum connection offers a pathway to personal growth, fulfilment, and success.

The Ripple Effect of Connection

Perhaps most importantly, these examples highlight the ripple effect of connection, the way in which our individual actions and intentions reverberate outward, influencing the collective consciousness of humanity and shaping the course of history. By aligning ourselves with the power of connection and intention, we become agents of change, co-creating a more harmonious and sustainable world for future generations.

Pay It Forward Movement: In 2000, a middle school teacher in California launched a simple yet powerful initiative known as the "Pay It Forward" movement. He challenged his students to perform acts of kindness for others without expecting anything in return, with the only request being that they pass on the goodwill to others. The idea quickly spread beyond the classroom, inspiring individuals and communities worldwide to perform random acts of kindness. From paying for a stranger's coffee to volunteering at local shelters, these small acts of kindness created a ripple effect of compassion and generosity, touching the lives of countless people and fostering a sense of interconnectedness and community spirit.

Community Garden Project: In a neighbourhood struggling with social isolation and environmental degradation, a group of residents came together to create a community garden project. Through collaborative efforts, they transformed a vacant lot into a thriving green space where neighbours could gather, grow fresh produce, and connect with nature and each other. As the garden flourished, it became a focal point for community events, educational workshops, and volunteer opportunities, fostering a sense of belonging and empowerment among residents. The positive impact of the community garden extended beyond its physical boundaries, inspiring neighboring communities to launch similar projects and catalysing a broader movement towards urban sustainability and social cohesion.

Quantum connection is not just a theoretical concept; it is a transformative force that shapes our reality and influences the course of human history. By harnessing the power of connection and intention, we can manifest our desires, foster resilience, and create positive change in our lives and communities. And through our collective efforts to honour the principles of quantum connection, we can co-create a world where all beings thrive in harmony, abundance, and well-being.

In the grand tapestry of existence, amidst the dance of particles and waves, there exists a profound truth, a truth that transcends the boundaries of space and time, a truth known as quantum connection. We will reflect on the importance of embracing quantum connection as a guiding principle for personal and collective evolution, and we encourage the cultivation of a sense of unity, compassion, and interconnectedness in daily life.

Recognising the Importance of Quantum Connection

At its core, quantum connection is the recognition that we are not separate from the universe, but integral parts of a larger whole. It is the understanding that beneath the illusion of separateness lies a deeper truth, a truth that binds all beings together in a web of cosmic kinship. By endorsing quantum connection, we awaken to the inherent unity and interconnectedness of all things, transcending the limitations of the individual self and tapping into a deeper source of inspiration and support.

Cultivating Unity and Compassion in Daily Life

In our daily lives, the practice of embracing quantum connection begins with cultivating a sense of unity, compassion, and interconnectedness with all beings. It is about recognising the inherent worth and dignity of every individual, and treating others with kindness, empathy, and respect. By extending our circle of compassion beyond the boundaries of the individual self, we create a ripple effect of positive change that reverberates throughout the fabric of reality.

Tapping into a Deeper Source of Inspiration and Support

By embracing quantum connection, we tap into a deeper source of inspiration and support, a source that transcends the limitations of the individual ego and aligns us with the flow of the universe. It is a source of wisdom, creativity, and intuition, a wellspring of guidance and insight that guides us on the path of personal and collective evolution. By trusting in this deeper source of support, we find the courage to step into our highest potential and co-create a world of harmony, abundance, and well-being for all beings.

Embracing the Power of Quantum Connection

In conclusion, embracing quantum connection is not just a philosophical concept; it is a transformative practice that has the power to shape our reality and influence the course of human history. By cultivating a sense of unity, compassion, and interconnectedness in daily life, we tap into a deeper source of inspiration and support that empowers us to realise our highest aspirations and co-create a world of harmony and well-being. And through our collective efforts to honour the principles of quantum connection, we can usher in a new era of personal and collective evolution, where all beings thrive in unity, love, and abundance.

Conclusion

As we reach the culmination of our journey through the realms of quantum physics and personal development, it's time to pause and reflect on the transformative path we've traversed. From the depths of quantum mechanics to the heights of self-discovery, we've delved into the mysteries of the universe and unlocked the hidden potential within ourselves. In this concluding chapter, we recall key insights, lessons learned, and moments of growth experienced throughout our exploration of "Quantum Manifestation: Harnessing Physics for Self-Improvement."

Embracing Quantum Principles for Personal Growth

Our journey began with an exploration of the quantum realm, a realm where uncertainty reigns, and potentiality abounds. We discovered that at the quantum level, our thoughts and intentions have the power to shape our reality, and that by harnessing the principles of quantum physics, we can become conscious creators of our destiny. We learned to embrace uncertainty as a catalyst for growth, and to cultivate a mindset of abundance, possibility, and resilience in the face of life's challenges.

Unveiling the Power of Mindfulness and Intention

Along our journey, we delved into the transformative practices of mindfulness and intention, a journey inward to explore the depths of our own consciousness and unlock the hidden potential within. We discovered that by cultivating present-moment awareness and aligning our intentions with our deepest desires and aspirations, we can manifest our dreams into reality and create a life of purpose, fulfilment, and joy.

Navigating the Interconnected Web of Existence

As we journeyed deeper into the heart of quantum manifestation, we studied the profound interconnectedness of all things, a web of cosmic kinship that binds us together in a tapestry of unity and love. We learned that by recognising our interconnectedness with the universe and all its inhabitants, we tap into a deeper source of inspiration and support that empowers us to realise our highest potential and co-create a world of harmony and well-being.

Celebrating Growth, Resilience, and Transformation

Throughout our exploration, we encountered moments of growth, resilience, and transformation, moments that challenged us to step outside our comfort zones, confront our fears, and embrace our inherent worth and power. We learned that growth is a lifelong journey, a journey of self-discovery, self-expression, and self-empowerment that unfolds with each passing moment.

Embracing the Journey of Quantum Manifestation

Let us remember that the power to shape our reality lies within us, that we are the architects of our own destiny, the creators of our own reality. Let us embrace uncertainty as a doorway to possibility, and cultivate a mindset of abundance, resilience, and joy in every moment. And let us continue to walk the path of personal growth and self-discovery with courage, curiosity, and an open heart, knowing that the journey itself is the destination, the journey of quantum manifestation, where physics meets self-improvement, and the infinite potential of the universe becomes our playground for exploration and transformation.

As we come to the close of our exploration through the realms of quantum manifestation, it's time to recognise and embrace the profound truth that lies at the heart of our journey, the truth that each of us possesses an inherent power, a power to shape our reality through the thoughts we think, the beliefs we hold, and the actions we take. We emphasise the inherent potential within each individual to harness this power and encourage you to recognise your agency as quantum creators, taking ownership of their lives and manifesting their highest aspirations into reality.

Awakening to Our Creative Potential

Throughout our journey, we've looked into the mysteries of quantum physics and discovered that at the deepest level of reality, we are not merely passive observers, but active participants in the co-creation of our destiny. We've learned that our thoughts and intentions have the power to shape the fabric of reality, and that by aligning ourselves with the principles of quantum physics, we can become conscious creators of our own lives.

Embracing Our Role as Quantum Creators

As we reflect on the insights gained and lessons learned along our journey, let us embrace our role as quantum creators and take ownership of our lives. Let us recognise that we are not victims of circumstance, but architects of our own destiny, that we have the power to transform our reality by harnessing the power of our thoughts, beliefs, and actions.

Cultivating a Mindset of Empowerment and Possibility

In the face of life's challenges and uncertainties, let us cultivate a mindset of empowerment and possibility, a mindset that recognises the infinite potential within us and the boundless opportunities that lie ahead. Let us release self-limiting beliefs and embrace the belief that anything is possible, that we can achieve our wildest dreams and aspirations.

Taking Inspired Action and Creating Positive Change

As we embark on the next chapter of our journey, let us remember that manifestation is not just about wishing and waiting, but about taking inspired action and co-creating our reality with the universe. Let us take bold steps toward our goals, fuelled by the knowledge that we are supported by the infinite wisdom and intelligence of the cosmos.

Empowering Ourselves to Thrive

Let us harness the power within and empower ourselves to thrive. Let us recognise our agency as quantum creators and take ownership of our lives, knowing that we have the power to shape our reality and manifest our highest aspirations into being. And let us continue to walk the path of personal growth and self-discovery with courage, curiosity, and an unwavering belief in the limitless potential of the human spirit.

It's time to bridge the gap between theory and practice, to provide guidance on how to apply the principles of quantum physics and personal development in everyday life.

Setting Clear Intentions

The first step in applying the principles of quantum manifestation is to set clear intentions for what you want to create in your life. Take some time to reflect on your deepest desires and aspirations and write them down in a clear and concise manner. By clarifying your intentions, you create a roadmap for manifestation and align yourself with the flow of the universe.

Cultivating Mindfulness and Presence

Mindfulness is a powerful practice that allows you to cultivate present-moment awareness and tap into the infinite potential of the quantum realm. Incorporate mindfulness exercises into your daily routine, such as meditation, deep breathing, or mindful movement. By cultivating presence, you become more attuned to the subtle energies and synchronicities that guide you on your path.

Practicing Visualisation and Affirmation

Visualisation and affirmation are potent tools for harnessing the power of your subconscious mind and aligning yourself with your desired outcomes. Take time each day to visualise yourself achieving your goals with clarity and vivid detail. Use affirmations to reinforce positive beliefs and reprogram your subconscious mind for success.

Taking Inspired Action

Manifestation is not just about wishing and waiting; it's about taking inspired action toward

your goals. Identify concrete steps you can take to move closer to your desired outcomes and commit to taking action consistently. Trust in the process and remain open to opportunities and synchronicities that arise along the way.

Embracing Gratitude and Surrender

Finally, cultivate an attitude of gratitude and surrender as you navigate the journey of manifestation. Express gratitude for the blessings and abundance already present in your life, and trust that the universe has your back. Surrender attachment to outcomes and allow space for divine timing and intervention.

Empowering Yourself to Manifest Your Dreams

By applying the principles of quantum physics and personal development in your everyday life, you empower yourself to manifest your dreams and create a life of purpose, fulfilment, and joy. Set clear intentions, cultivate mindfulness and presence, practice visualisation and affirmation, take inspired action, and embrace gratitude and surrender. By integrating these principles into your daily routines and manifestation practices, you tap into the infinite potential of the quantum realm and co-create a reality that aligns with your highest aspirations. Remember, you are the architect of your own destiny, the quantum creator of your reality. Embrace your power and unleash your potential to manifest the life of your dreams.

Embracing Curiosity as a Catalyst for Growth

Curiosity is the spark that ignites the flame of exploration and discovery, it is the driving force behind our quest for knowledge, understanding, and self-discovery. By embracing curiosity, we open ourselves up to new experiences, perspectives, and possibilities, enriching our lives and expanding our horizons in profound ways.

Cultivating Wonder and Awe

In the hustle and bustle of modern life, it's easy to lose sight of the magic and wonder that surrounds us each day. Yet, by cultivating a sense of wonder and awe, we reconnect with the beauty and mystery of the world around us, tapping into a deep wellspring of inspiration and creativity that fuels our journey of self-discovery and personal growth.

Embracing Lifelong Learning and Exploration

Learning is a lifelong journey, a journey of exploration, discovery, and growth that extends far beyond the confines of formal education. By embracing lifelong learning, we nourish our minds, expand our horizons, and cultivate a spirit of curiosity and openness that enriches every aspect of our lives.

Embracing the Journey of Self-Discovery

As you continue on your journey of self-discovery and personal growth, remember to cultivate curiosity, wonder, and openness to new possibilities. Embrace each day as an opportunity for exploration and learning, and approach life with a sense of childlike wonder and awe. By embracing curiosity and openness, you tap into the infinite potential of the quantum realm and co-create a reality that is rich with possibility and potential. And through your journey of lifelong learning and exploration, you empower yourself to evolve, grow, and thrive in alignment with your highest aspirations. You may you continue to embrace the journey with an open heart and a curious mind, knowing that the path of self-discovery is endless, and the possibilities are infinite.

Let us reflect on the invaluable role of courage in the face of challenges and acknowledge the inevitability of obstacles and setbacks on the journey of personal development. Inspire yourself to cultivate courage, resilience, and perseverance in the face of adversity, knowing that challenges are opportunities for growth.

Embracing the Journey of Personal Development

The journey of personal development is not always smooth sailing, it is often marked by twists and turns, ups and downs, challenges, and setbacks. Yet, it is through facing these challenges that we grow, evolve, and become the best versions of ourselves. As we reflect on our own journeys, let us acknowledge the inevitability of challenges and setbacks, and recognise them as integral parts of the process of personal growth and evolution.

Cultivating Courage and Resilience

In the face of adversity, courage is our greatest ally, it is the inner strength that allows us to face our fears, overcome obstacles, and persevere in the pursuit of our dreams. Cultivate courage by stepping outside your comfort zone, taking risks, and embracing the unknown. And when setbacks arise, draw upon your resilience, the ability to bounce back from adversity stronger and more determined than ever before.

Finding Opportunity in Adversity

Challenges are not roadblocks, but opportunities for growth, they push us to stretch beyond our limits, expand our horizons, and discover our true potential. Instead of fearing challenges, embrace them as opportunities for learning, self-discovery, and transformation. Approach each obstacle with an open heart and a curious mind, knowing that within every challenge lies the seed of opportunity.

Embracing the Journey with Courage and Resilience

As you continue your journey of personal development and self-improvement, remember to cultivate courage, resilience, and perseverance in the face of challenges. Acknowledge the inevitability of obstacles and setbacks, but do not let them deter you from pursuing your dreams. Instead, approach challenges with courage and determination, knowing that they are opportunities for growth and transformation. And through your courage and resilience, may you overcome any obstacle that stands in your way and emerge stronger, wiser, and more empowered than ever before. Embrace the journey with courage and resilience, knowing that with every challenge you face, you have the opportunity to become the person you were always meant to be.

The Inherent Support of the Universe

At the heart of quantum manifestation lies the understanding that we are not alone in the journey of self-improvement and personal growth. The universe, with its infinite wisdom and intelligence, is always conspiring in our favour, guiding us along the path of our highest potential. In times of doubt and uncertainty, remember that you are supported by the vastness of the cosmos, and that you are never alone on your journey.

Embracing the Unfolding of Life's Journey

Life is a journey, a journey of discovery, growth, and evolution. Along the way, we encounter twists and turns, ups and downs, moments of joy and moments of challenge. Embrace the unfolding of life's journey with an open heart and a curious mind, trusting that every experience has its purpose and every obstacle its lesson. In the midst of uncertainty, trust in the process of life, knowing that everything is unfolding exactly as it should.

Faith in the Greater Intelligence and Purpose

Beyond the chaos and complexity of the world lies a greater intelligence and purpose at work, an intelligence that transcends our understanding and a purpose that guides the unfolding of the cosmos. Have faith in this greater intelligence and purpose, knowing that everything happens for a reason and that you are exactly where you are meant to be in this moment. Trust in the divine orchestration of the universe and surrender to the flow of life with grace and humility.

Surrendering to the Wisdom of the Universe

As you continue on your journey of self-discovery and personal growth, remember to trust the universe. Trust in the inherent support and guidance available from the cosmos and have faith in the unfolding of life's journey. Surrender to the greater intelligence and purpose at work, knowing that you are supported by the wisdom of the universe every step of the way. And through your trust and surrender, may you find peace, joy, and fulfilment in the unfolding of your destiny. Trust the universe and let the wisdom of the cosmos guide you on the journey of a lifetime.

Embracing the Beauty of the Journey

Life is a journey, a journey of self-discovery, growth, and transformation. Along the way, we encounter challenges and triumphs, joys and sorrows, moments of clarity and moments of confusion. Embrace the beauty of the journey with an open heart and a curious mind, knowing that every experience has its purpose, and every step forward brings you closer to your highest potential.

Celebrating Progress and Success

As you navigate the twists and turns of your personal journey, take time to celebrate your progress and success. Celebrate the small victories and milestones along the way, acknowledging the courage, resilience, and determination that have brought you to this moment. By celebrating progress, you honour your journey and fuel your motivation to continue moving forward with passion and purpose.

Enjoying the Process of Growth and Evolution

In the pursuit of personal growth and manifestation, it's easy to become fixated on the end goal and overlook the beauty of the process itself. Embrace the journey with a sense of joy and wonder, savouring each moment and embracing the lessons and experiences that come your way. Find joy in the journey of self-discovery, growth, and evolution, knowing that every step forward brings you closer to your dreams.

Staying Committed to Personal Evolution

Finally, as you continue on your journey of self-discovery and manifestation, stay committed to personal evolution. Keep an open mind and a willing heart, remaining curious, adaptable, and resilient in the face of challenges and opportunities. Trust in the process of growth and change, knowing that every experience, whether positive or negative, is an opportunity for learning and transformation.

Embracing the Journey with Gratitude and Grace

Appreciate the journey of self-discovery, growth, and manifestation with gratitude and grace. Celebrate the beauty of the journey, enjoy the process of growth and evolution, and stay committed to personal transformation. And through your journey, may you discover the true essence of who you are and unleash the limitless potential that resides within. So, dear reader, embrace the journey with an open heart and a willing spirit, knowing that the greatest adventure of all is the journey of self-discovery and personal evolution.

Let us reflect on the profound significance of connection and community in the journey of self-improvement, as we highlight the importance of cultivating connection and community, and encourage you to seek support, share experiences, and collaborate with others on their path to personal growth.

The Power of Connection in Manifestation

Connection is at the heart of the manifestation journey, it is the invisible thread that binds us together in a web of cosmic kinship, and the catalyst for co-creating our reality with the universe. By cultivating connection with ourselves, with others, and with the world around us, we tap into a deeper source of inspiration and support that empowers us to manifest our dreams into reality.

Finding Support and Guidance in Community

In the journey of self-improvement, community is our greatest ally, it is the tribe of like-minded souls who lift us up, inspire us, and hold space for our growth and evolution. Seek out community, whether online or in-person, where you can share your experiences, ask for support, and receive guidance from others who are walking a similar path. Together, we amplify our collective intention and create a ripple effect of positive change in the world.

Collaboration and Co-Creation

Collaboration is the key to unlocking the full potential of manifestation, it is the art of coming together with others to co-create a reality that is greater than the sum of its parts. Collaborate with others on your path to personal growth, whether through mastermind groups, workshops,

or creative projects. By pooling our resources, talents, and insights, we accelerate our collective evolution and create a world of harmony and abundance for all.

Embracing Connection and Community

Clasp onto the power of connection and community in your journey of self-improvement and manifestation. Seek out support, share your experiences, and collaborate with others on your path to personal growth. By cultivating connection and community, we tap into a deeper source of inspiration and support that empowers us to manifest our dreams into reality and co-create a world of harmony and well-being for all. Remember that you are not alone on your journey, reach out, connect, and together, let us manifest a brighter future for ourselves and for the world.

The Power of Gratitude in Manifestation

Gratitude is a potent force that has the power to transform our lives from the inside out. When we cultivate a sense of gratitude and appreciation for the abundance and blessings present in our lives, we shift our focus from what is lacking to what is abundant, from what is wrong to what is right. In doing so, we align ourselves with the flow of the universe and open ourselves up to receiving even more blessings and abundance in return.

Cultivating a Daily Gratitude Practice

One of the most powerful ways to harness the transformative power of gratitude is through a daily gratitude practice. Take a few moments each day to reflect on the things you are grateful for, whether it's the love of family and friends, the beauty of nature, or the simple pleasures of life. Write them down in a gratitude journal or simply say them out loud. By cultivating a daily gratitude practice, you train your mind to focus on the positive and attract more of what you desire into your life.

Embracing the Abundance Mindset

Gratitude is not just about being thankful for what you have; it's about embracing an abundance mindset, a mindset that recognises the infinite possibilities and opportunities that abound in every moment. When we approach life with a mindset of abundance, we attract more abundance into our lives, creating a positive feedback loop of prosperity and well-being.

Living a Life of Gratitude and Appreciation

Cultivate a sense of gratitude and appreciation for the abundance and blessings present in your life. Embrace a daily gratitude practice as a way of fostering positivity and attracting more of what you desire. By living a life of gratitude and appreciation, you align yourself with the flow of the universe and open yourself up to receiving even more blessings and abundance in return. Take a moment to reflect on the things you are grateful for, and let gratitude be your guiding light on the journey of self-improvement and manifestation.

As we reach the end of our journey through the realms of quantum manifestation, I offer you these final words of encouragement, inspiration, and empowerment. May they serve as a guiding light on your path as you continue your journey of self-improvement and manifestation.

You Are Limitless Potential

You are a being of limitless potential, capable of achieving anything you set your mind to. Believe in yourself and your ability to manifest the life of your dreams. You are more powerful than you realise, and the universe is conspiring in your favour every step of the way.

Trust in the Process

Trust in the process of manifestation and the unfolding of your journey. Know that everything is happening exactly as it should, and that every experience, whether positive or negative, is guiding you toward your highest good. Trust in the support and guidance of the universe and surrender to the flow of life with grace and humility.

Embrace the Journey with Courage and Resilience

Embrace the journey with courage and resilience, knowing that challenges are opportunities for growth and setbacks are merely detours on the path to success. Have faith in your ability to overcome any obstacle that stands in your way, and trust in your inner strength and resilience to carry you through even the darkest of times.

You Are Never Alone

Remember that you are never alone on your journey. The universe is always with you, supporting you, guiding you, and cheering you on every step of the way. Trust in the divine orchestration of the cosmos, and know that you are loved, supported, and cherished beyond measure.

Believe in Yourself and Your Dreams

Believe in yourself and your ability to manifest the life of your dreams. You are a powerful co-creator of your reality, and the universe is your willing partner in the journey of self-improvement and manifestation. Trust in the process, embrace the journey with courage and resilience, and know that you are never alone. Go forth with confidence, knowing that the power to create the life you desire lies within you. Believe in yourself, believe in your dreams, and let your light shine brightly for all the world to see.

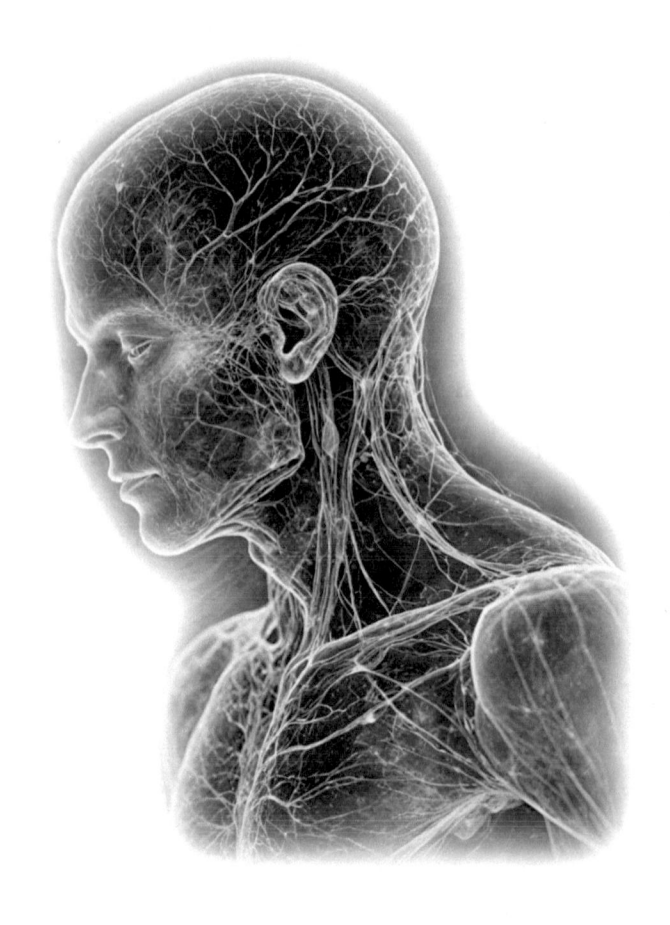

Thank you for reading Quantum Manifestation:

Harnessing Physics for Self-Improvement

Made in the USA
Columbia, SC
17 July 2025